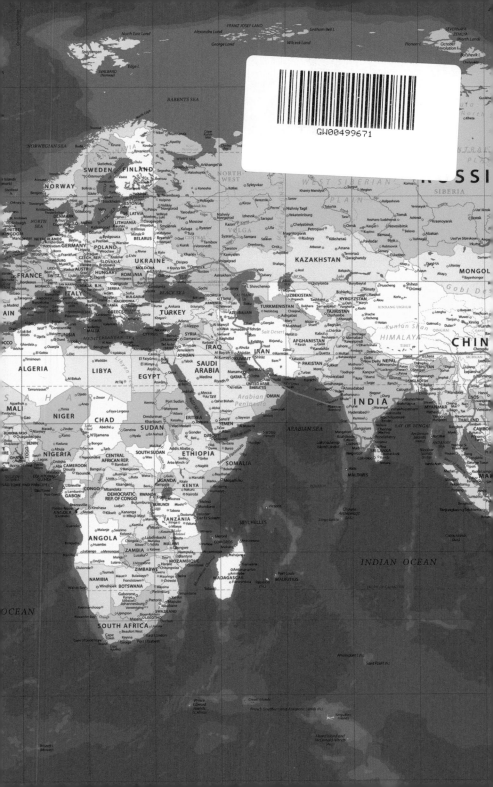

WINGING IT

A Drive Around the World

HICKY BACON
& TOM HOWARD

First published in Great Britain in 2021 by Singhdog
Publishing Corporation

Edited, designed and produced by Tandem Publishing
http://tandempublishing.yolasite.com/

ISBN: 978-1-3999-0521-3

10 9 8 7 6 5 4 3 2 1

A CIP catalogue record for this book is available from the
British Library.

To Netty Hedges of the British Red Cross

Acknowledgements

Foley Specialist Vehicles – for finding Netty and preparing her so brilliantly that she didn't let us down once on the entire trip.

The British Red Cross – without which we would never have met Netty's inspiring namesake, Netty Hedges.

The team at CR: Terry, Mike and David – for doing their bit to kit out Netty with wooden trunks and metal cages, and for last-minute logistics.

Count Kálnoky – for hosting us in Romania and sharing his passion for that wonderful country.

Johnny Hornby – for so generously stepping in not only to fix, but to fund, our increasingly desperate attempts to ship Netty across both the Arabian Sea and the Pacific.

The Kumar Family – our hosts in Calcutta and lifelong friends.

Chiran Shumsher Thapa – our host in Kathmandu and custodian of Netty as we headed for Everest.

Dickie D'Abo – for housing us in LA as we waited for Netty to be released from the evil clutches of US Customs. A somewhat longer stay than expected!

And lastly to the family, friend and girlfriend who joined us at intervals along the way.

Contents

PROLOGUE

Hatched

Tom

It is 11:32am on Tuesday October 13th 2009 and, waving to thousands of adoring family and friends, we are circling Parliament Square in London. Traffic is unusually light. We pass Churchill's statue, the old boy looking stooped but somehow noble in the bright autumnal sun. Just the sort of day for beginnings. Surely the auspices are good.

I forage in the glove box and pull out our small pile of essential documents. 'Passports. Yours. Mine.'

'Check,' says Hicky, grinning at me from behind the wheel.

'Carnet?' The passport for the car, this vital document would authorise the passage of our vehicle through nearly every country on the globe. I look at Hicky. 'Wait – where's the bloody carnet?'

'Shit,' he mutters.

~

It was the recession that brought all this together. I suppose it had to be good for something. The idea that I needed to do something substantial, something big, and – most importantly – something challenging, had grown to a point that I could no longer ignore. I can't remember exactly when it crystallised into a desire to drive around the world, but the kernel had been there throughout three somewhat under-utilised years of university. Certainly by the time I started my first job working for Knox D'Arcy, a firm of management consultants, I must have known I would do something like this. When I signed my contract I somehow negotiated into it, in principle, that I would be permitted a sabbatical after only two years in the job. Amazing cheek, when I think of it now, and more amazing that they agreed. In principle.

The consultant's lifestyle of hotel rooms five nights a week may have been miserable but I did find the work I was doing interesting. Then, in the autumn of 2008 the Financial Crisis hit. I moved back to London where at least the social life was more appealing, but the work tailed off. The markets slowed and most of the interesting work the firm had been doing simply dried up. Productivity dwindled. It was pretty soul-destroying. It seemed the cold winds of market forces had blown my career onto a sandbar. The more frustrated I felt, the more the ties that had bound me to my desk and my career began to loosen and my mind cast around for the next new challenge. An old day-dream – which I had been knocking about with a friend for some time already – loomed larger in my imagination.

To drive around the world.

Soon it was all I could think about.

Hicky

Tom first pitched the idea to me over an après-ski beer in a bar called the Balmalp, perched high up above Zürs on an Austrian mountain. It was a beautiful clear day and we were drunk.

'But we don't know the first thing about driving round the world,' I laughed.

'How hard can it be?' Seeing my doubtful look, he added, 'We could learn on the job.'

'Winging it, you mean.'

'Exactly,' he grinned wolfishly. 'Winging it.'

At 2,000m above sea level, the Balmalp always was a place for outlandish dreams. I gazed out over the sun-lit peaks to a horizon that stretched for miles and miles. My head was light with the view or the altitude or more probably the Stiegl, but just then the idea didn't seem as crazy as it doubtless should. I clinked his glass with mine. 'I'm in.'

That was March 2009. I was approaching the end of a year at Cass Business School in London where I was studying for a masters in property. I still had no idea what I wanted to do long term. I'd had a couple of jobs after leaving university, in property and marketing, for the couple of years prior to Cass, but nothing that felt like a vocation. The idea behind going to Cass was to add some professional theory to the practice. But then the world collapsed. The Financial Crisis hit during the autumn I had enrolled. And now, with the end of my masters fast approaching and the prospect of gainful employment in any area of interest looking depressingly thin, a year of expanding my horizons at the wheel of a 4x4 began to look like quite a sensible option. I had never travelled much, apart from a six-month internship living in New

York – which hardly reached the realm of wild adventure. I had the feeling that this could be my last chance before life got more serious. I wanted to get out of my bubble and understand the world. Not just read about a place but see it and dispel whatever theories or images someone else would have me believe.

I was ready to do it.

Towards the end of March, Tom and I met for dinner in the Marquis of Granby on Romney Street in Westminster to discuss it further. Afterwards we went back to Tom's flat where we cracked open a couple of beers, pulled out his *Times World Atlas* and started looking at routes. Our only real criterion was to maximise the number of countries we visited, while avoiding as far as possible anywhere we had been before. The funny thing is, the route we came up with that night in that rather slap-dash fashion ended up being almost exactly the route we followed.

Tom

After that, there was a lull. We realised our ambitions would only really crystallise once we had to lay down some money. Through the spring we did a bit of research into overland vehicles, eventually zero-ing in on a company called Foley's based in Essex. This family-run outfit acted as an agency for this sort of expedition. They would find and sell us a car and then fit it out with everything required to pull off our round-the-world tour. We told our contact there, Fergie, that we had a budget of twelve thousand pounds. He was nonplussed, to say the least. He claimed this was the smallest budget he'd ever dealt with, but we were insistent: we wanted a finished car, entirely 'speck'ed' out for that money. In the end, he found us an old utility vehicle, a 1999 Land Rover Defender 110 300 Tdi, previous owner Leicestershire County Council, that had 192,000 miles on the clock, all done on motorways and which would cost us the princely sum of £3,950 plus VAT.

That was the first moment when we had to put our money where our mouths were. The next was when I had to quit my job towards the end of June. My boss seemed genuinely disappointed and tried to tempt me to stay by dangling the offer of a project in Los Angeles and New York under my nose. It sounded like a great job. Out of courtesy to him I said I'd consider it, and I did for a while, but I soon concluded there would be other great jobs. This, however, was the opportunity of a lifetime. My mind was made up.

We spent that summer getting ready. Although, when you read about the meticulous preparations of other overland expeditions, by comparison ours was rather … well, *laissez-faire*. Hicky bought the maps we needed from Stanfords on Long Acre. I bought a book about Land Rover motor maintenance.

Neither of us knew anything at all about the inner workings of a motor engine, but rather than complete a full motor maintenance course, Fergie said we could spend a day with one of their mechanics. This we duly did: completely and utterly pointless. It entailed shadowing a miniature version of Hagrid the giant as he described his dream overland trip in agonising detail, whilst simultaneously extracting some tiny part from the heart of a totally different model's engine. The procedure was utterly irrelevant to anything we might actually need to know and quite beyond our capabilities anyway. We left none the wiser, but made damn sure we had Foley's phone number.

Hicky

We took first aid a bit more seriously. I say 'we' – Tom did, anyway. I had become preoccupied with the logistical headache of shipping our vehicle across the Persian Gulf while trying to dream up names for our website. Some of the names in the running were:

- East2east.co.uk
- Hickyandtom.com (which had a better ring to it)
- Tomandhicky.com
- Norfolkingchance.com

even

- expandingthenorfolkgenepool.com

(In case you hadn't guessed it we are both from Nelson's county.) In the end we settled on the more innocuous 'Hicky and Tom's Blog'.

We did a four-day first-aid course with an amazing lady called Netty Hedges of the British Red Cross, who tried to teach us all we needed to know while fussing over us and moaning about 'bloody modern regulations'. She particularly objected to the IV solution she was required to recommend, convinced her own home brew was considerably better. She had suffered several strokes herself, but was still going strong at eighty-six. With that in mind, we ended up calling our Land Rover 'Netty' – figuring that naming the thing after an old girl with a few miles on the clock who refuses to give up was rather appropriate. By the end of the four days, Tom was quite an accomplished first-aider. Me, not so much. 'It's pretty clear who needs to have the accident,' Tom observed.

Through September the car was nearly ready and I was responsible for sorting out a bank account and all the necessary visas for our route. This was done in idiosyncratically nonchalant style – a style for which 'winging it' soon came to be the catch-all term. Tom happened to make an off-the-cuff remark to me one day that we should probably make a start on the visa process, after which we ran them back-to-back. Iran was a tough one, I remember, but in the end we obtained the final visa needed on the day before we were due to leave, which was October 13th 2009. Perfect timing, by pure fluke.

Meanwhile, Foley's had been speck'ing out Netty, our trusty vehicle. Wanting to keep the budget as low as we could, we wrangled over pretty much every single piece of kit, deciding whether to include it or not. We had to concede on a couple of practical things, whilst losing some of the more aesthetically fun options. For instance, Fergie convinced us we definitely *did* need a bar across the back door to support our spare wheel – but that we probably did not need one of those awesome-looking winches that mount on the front bumper. Shame. In the end, the final bill came in at £13,466 which included the following modifications:

- Hidden engine immobiliser switch
- Safe under the passenger footwell
- Additional long-range fuel tanks
- Side compartments for jerry cans of fuel
- Water tank and tap on the rear fender
- Reinforced suspension
- New tyres
- Supporting arm for spare tyre
- Roof rack

- Roof tent
- Extra batteries and power inverter for powering appliances when camping
- Reinforced steel rings on rear door for padlocking shut

We spent a morning with them, during which they walked us through the various pieces of kit, as well as things to know about Netty herself. Our favourite item was undoubtedly the tent, which was stowed on the roof and unfolded like a children's pop-up book, complete with a built-in mattress. Beautifully designed, it was to prove its mettle on countless occasions. Apart from that, I can't say we concentrated that hard. By now, our principle of 'winging it' had become our default position and we thought most of what Fergie told us was self-explanatory anyhow.

Alongside this, there was a bit of desk work to be done – researching some of the places we intended to visit, corresponding with whatever contacts we could muster along the way, plotting the route in greater detail, even sorting the official government guide who would accompany us across China. And of course, the big one – arranging Netty's voyage by sea from Bandar Abbas to Mumbai. This last was to prove a massive headache and, the closer we got to Iran, it became our biggest source of anxiety, even though we had the head of operations for DP World on the job for us. But more on that later.

Tom
As well as Foley's work on Netty, we had arranged for a carpenter from our home county of Norfolk to make

some storage units to be installed in the back to help us stay vaguely organised. We also had a detachable security cage built (again in Norfolk) that could be padlocked in such a way to separate the cab of the Land Rover from the storage space in the back. Since the rear of the Land Rover had no windows the most vulnerable point of entry was the cab. This meant that if anyone did manage to break into the front they would only get what few items we had left there but they would be very unlikely to be able to break into the rear. Netty (or 'the Netster') herself had a secret immobiliser switch which we would come to use religiously and which made her a much tougher target than your average Defender.

By now, our departure date was approaching fast. I was nervous – well, more excited than nervous, really – and wanting to get on with it. Wanting to see what was going to happen. We were still waiting for our passports from the Indian Embassy which was our last visa application. Cutting it fine, we had been told these would be ready for collection on October 12th, a Monday and the day before departure. On the Friday beforehand, we had a bit of a send-off party in a very forgettable place off Regent Street called the Moose Bar. It was fun – about fifty friends or so – a few of whom said they expected we'd be back within a couple of weeks with our tails between our legs. I smiled and laughed with them, whilst inside I was thinking, 'No chance we're letting that happen!'

We both caught the train up to Norfolk, where the car was awaiting *le grand départ*. Instinctively, we wanted to spend our last weekend with our respective families. However, I awoke on Sunday morning to find Netty looking rather sheepish, sitting on top of a fresh puddle of diesel. Clearly something was seriously wrong. I called up Fergie in a bit of a panic, explaining at high speed and in a rather shrill voice that the car was broken.

After I described the problem, he said it must be a leak in the link between the main fuel tanks and the 120-litre long-range tank that they had installed.

'If you can get it down to us today, we'll get it fixed for you.'

'In time for Tuesday?'

'Oh – sure, sure.'

We still had a lot of packing to do so a friend kindly volunteered to drive Netty down to Foley's. Meanwhile, Hicky and I returned to London to the flat to complete our packing, do final checks on our inventory and await that last visa. True to his word, Fergie had the car back to us remarkably swiftly, but then, within only a matter of hours, Netty had leaked a second time. We couldn't help but think it horribly ominous.

Our hearts were in our mouths as our friend David was despatched a *second* time to Essex. Foley's must have fixed it on the same day because I remember trying to enjoy our final farewell dinner on the Monday night with parents (and girlfriend, in my case), while really all I could think about was whether the car would be ready. Late that night, and to a huge sigh of relief, Netty was delivered safely back, ready for the off the following morning.

So there we were. On a blazing blue October morning in Parliament Square. Our passports had been collected from the Indian Embassy. Netty was packed, complete with spare parts, tent, clothing (for hot and cold), sleeping bags, books, dried food, a few choice bottles of wine, camping stove and all its accoutrements, and bags of various 'British' paraphernalia – flags, hats, boxes of Tetley teabags and the like (for distribution) – as well as a myriad of other bits and bobs.

There was some gentle piping of the eyes by the parents (well, mothers, anyway) and then we were off, with a wave of the hand, a toot of the horn and a yawning pit in the stomach, at 11:30am on the dot.

By 11:33 we had already been reminded just how green we were by discovering that we had forgotten Netty's carnet. Two circuits of Parliament Square and some frantic scrabbling through the glove box and it was back to the flat, grab the stupid thing and off we set again, feeling a little less like the intrepid overlanders than we had before, but hugely relieved nonetheless.

I can't recall much about the drive to the Eurotunnel, other than it was a beautiful, clear morning, an easy run down to Folkestone and we didn't talk much. But once we were loaded and the windows darkened as we entered the tunnel, we both agreed the welter of emotions had coalesced into just one:

Pure excitement.

Wings spread wide, we were gone.

ONE

Fledglings

Hicky

It is a bright day as we debouch from the Eurotunnel train onto the first tarmac of the Eurasian landmass.

We settle into a few solid hours on the autoroute, motoring south at a steady 62mph over the great rolling plain of Northern France. (Incidentally 62mph was also the cruising speed of the 1955 Land Rover Defender used by the Oxford and Cambridge teams – the so-called 'First Overlanders' – in their famous trip from London to Singapore. Nothing changes and their story is well worth a read.) There's a bittersweet feeling to leaving England behind us now, but at the same time a certain relief that we are at last getting on with it.

We speed through a land scarred by the ravages of the Great War, past names recalled from history books (and *Blackadder Goes Forth*): Saint-Omer, Cambrai, Saint-Quentin. The scenes of those bloodbaths seem painfully close to the shores of England. It somehow feels appropriate that we stop for our first night at Camping Le Vivier aux Carpes, just south of Saint-Quentin, right in the heart of the Somme Valley.

It's dark. The place is deserted. The empty swings and slides give it all an eerie quality. It is October after all and hardly high season on the Riviera. The reviews have given us to expect an all-night serenade from the local frog population but, like the tourists, the frogs have gone elsewhere for the winter. Naturally there were teething problems when we started to unleash our camping knowledge, or lack thereof, on our unsuspecting equipment. Even our tent, which opened akin to a children's pop-up book, took multiple attempts and there is some question whether we can get the thing up at all. I feel slightly overwhelmed at the thought that we won't be back in the UK for another nine months at least, and even then we'll be approaching it from the west. Another hemisphere. By then, we'll be living proof that if you drive long enough in one direction you end up back where you started. A funny thought.

We venture out and find a kiosk that sells us a stale baguette and some cheese rind. Frugal beginnings, to say the least.

Tom
We sit down to eat, nerves still fluttering in my stomach. Can we really cope? We get the tent up eventually but then comes dinner. We peel off the wrapping around the small gas stove, insert the canister and are ready to go. Small problem – neither of us has either a lighter or any matches. Pretty basic stuff. Rather than traipse back to the shop we decide to see if there is anyone in the camp who can help us out. We knock on the nearest caravan door and our luck is in. A lovely English family lend us a lighter and politely ask us how long we are on holiday. We explain that this is the first day of a nine-month

journey around the world. They are suitably impressed and quickly tell us to keep the lighter as a memento. Returning to camp, we attempt to fire up the gas stove and nearly melt our faces off in the ensuing fireball we somehow manage to create. Slightly shaken we give up and resort to our sandwiches instead.

All of this takes place in virtual silence. The reality of what we are facing and first-day nerves are hitting home. I see my own malaise clearly reflected in Hicky's face as he looks back at me, face illuminated by the single bulb hanging off the side of the car. Luckily, he saves the day, disappearing into the back of the Land Rover, rummaging through his old school tuck box and reappearing with a magnum of Château Calon-Ségur 1989.

'A present from Dad,' he grins. 'Sort of see us on our way.'

This will become a theme that runs through our camping routine, at least most of the way through Europe and out its back door. Once we've seen away the bottle and the sandwiches are gone, our nerves settle down and there is nothing much to do but go to bed. It's 8pm.

The next day started well with a warmish shower, a brew a builder would be proud of and even fruit to appease the mothers. As we pull out of the campsite at the crack of dawn and turn the corner to pass our friendly neighbours, we find them leaning out of their windows waving and shouting good luck. It feels like a good omen and certainly bolsters our mood.

Driving on, the theme of the Great War continues. In the afternoon, we stop for a couple of hours to wander around the concrete behemoth that is the fortress memorial at Verdun. It's humbling. A hundred and thirty thousand men died here to preserve our freedom.

It certainly puts some sharp perspective on what we are doing and the rights we are exercising to achieve it.

Hicky is moved to take up smoking rolling tobacco. 'It'll give me something to do on the road.'

Hicky likes to keep busy, I suppose. The first aider in me wonders whether a commitment to red wine and cigarettes is the best way to begin a year of – let's be honest – mostly sitting on our backsides.

We were aiming, somewhat optimistically, to reach Lake Lucerne that evening, but after the extra time spent at the mesmerising Verdun this is not going to be possible.

A contingency plan is formed with military precision and we decide there is no better place to spend a night than in the Black Forest. At Strasbourg, we turn south, cross the Rhine and our first frontier, and cut down through a corner of the Black Forest itself. We leave the main route south and drive up a small valley to a village called Münstertal, nestled in the first foothills of the Schwarzwald and to another campsite.

As a result of our holidays in Austria, Hicky and I share a passion for sausage, or wurst in the mother tongue, and the Black Forest is famed for its 'Kielbasa Lesna'. This we duly sample in the local Gasthof. The waiter seems surprised when we tell him he's the second stop on a global tour.

'We'll send you a postcard down the road,' Hicky tells him. In return, he gives us each a glass of Germany's young fall wine or 'first harvest' wine, Federweisser, on the house. It tastes like semi-alcoholic grape juice but it's not at all bad.

Hicky
From there, we made good time, motoring down the east

side of Switzerland. Basel, Lucerne, Lugano and over the border into Italy to Lake Como. From our bible, the *AA Camping & Caravan 2009 Edition*, we settle on what it lovingly described as 'a well-kept site on the banks of the river'. In fact it is a depressing ghost town with not a living soul in sight. An empty swimming pool, reminiscent of the memorable scene in the Nicholas Cage classic *Con Air*, the most prominent feature. We take one look and instead opt for something a little more picturesque. Our first nudge into intrepidity pays off. We turn down a dirt track that leads right down to the shores of Lake Como. Much more like it. The water looks ball-achingly cold so we don't hazard a dip. Instead we are treated to a rather lovely sunset over the lake, resembling a Turner watercolour with the surrounding hilltops fading from brown to blue to black. As designated cook, I am beginning to hone what will become my signature dish: one-pot sausage cassoulet 'traditionnel'. (Essentially local sausage with tomato sauce and whatever condiments and spices are in my trunk.)

'Maybe we'll get the hang of this little thing they call overlanding after all,' I declare.

My cautious confidence is squashed like a fly on the windscreen the next morning when we stop to refuel Netty just over the border into Italy and discover a lake of oil beneath her.

Tom swears. 'Three days. We've lasted three days.'

We call up Fergie at Foley's and explain what we can see. He tells us the symptoms point to a crank-shaft oil-seal crack (whatever the hell that is). 'It's right in the centre of the engine.'

'How do you fix it?' Tom asks.

'You've got to take the whole engine apart.'

We exchange a look. I'm tasting the bitter bile of defeat, already imagining the look on my friends' faces when they find out we made it no further than Bergamo before we had to turn back. I swear I hear Fergie's chuckle over the phone.

'Well, what shall we do?' says Tom.

'I can send you a spare part to Vienna if you give me an address. But it's not easy to change. Best thing to do is just monitor it. Keep topping up the oil.'

'What? The whole way round the world?' I screech when Tom ends the call.

'That's what he says.'

Hmmm. I seriously consider buying shares in Castrol.

Day 4. A long day on the road. Our longest so far: 409 miles. Motorways all the way following the southern verge of the Dolomites, past Verona, Venice and Trieste, and then into Slovenia. We make a quick stop for a late lunch in Ljubljana where we play for the first time a game we christen 'Menu Roulette'. With no clue what anything on the menu says, I make a random selection from the list for a starter and then one for a main. What turns up are two plates of exactly the same sausage, one large and one small.

'Balls,' I say.

'I win, I think,' replies Tom, gazing down on my rather uninspiring meal. Other than that and the sight of a significant number of Chinese tourists (they get everywhere!), Ljubljana fails to dazzle.

Still, our vittles were sufficiently re-energising that Tom is inspired to take a smaller, more direct road to our target campsite once we are rolling again.

I am less inclined.

'It's clearly a short cut,' he says, having delved into our

extensive library of maps and picked out 'Eastern Europe, Colour Edition 2009'.

It is, of a sort. The road plunges into the woods and pushes straight up a forested hill before quickly dissolving into a dirt track. I am driving and throwing Netty around like Jeremy Clarkson after a night in a brewery. It's getting dark and I wonder out loud, in somewhat colourful terms, where the hell our campsite could be. Up till now we have not strayed from asphalt roads and this is the first time we have felt the real bite of adventure, of not knowing what lay ahead. The stress levels are rising in both of us.

Knowing that he's the better driver and, it's rapidly becoming apparent, a far weaker navigator, I let Tom take over. The whole thing feels edgy as the gloom thickens and the woods hemming us in seem more and more fore-boding as we continue up and up. At last we crest our first mountain pass – if you can call it that – and trundle down the other side where, sure enough, we find our destination. As we pull into the campsite dusk is rapidly dissolving into night. From what little we can see it is an immaculate place, far less desolate than the deserted campsites of France and Italy. But it's getting pretty cold. We settle for hot soup for supper. After a chilly night, we awake to a freezing morning and it's the first time we struggle to venture forth from our beds.

Tom

Vienna is, of course, beautiful.

Hicky has arranged for us to stay with a second cousin of his, whom he has never met before (and has never seen since, at the time of writing). She's about our age and very hospitable, but she lets us do all the tourist sights on our own. Neither of us have ever been to the Austrian capital before and we are impressed by the more obvious round of grand buildings: the StaatsOper, the Hofburg palace, Saint Stephen's Cathedral and the rest. But we've always got an eye down the road, in particular fixed on the window of time we have allocated for Iran, thanks to the dates on our visa. Any dawdling and there's a risk that our time in Iran will get squeezed. Thus, despite a fun and boozy night on the town, the three nights we have to spend in Vienna become frustrating. We are waiting for the part that Fergie said he'd send us from England. At last, it arrives at the second cousin's flat. We pop it in Netty's glove box, and there it will stay for the next 24,000 miles. Completely pointless, but I suppose knowing we have it does at least give us some reassurance, despite that neither of us has a clue what to do with it.

We set out down the grand boulevards of Vienna early on the morning of October 20th, heading east. Our destination for the day is Budapest which is only 160 miles away. We stop for lunch in Bratislava on the eastern bank of the Danube. I can't say the Slovakian capital leaves an indelible impression on the senses, especially after Vienna. However, over our sandwich, we declare a contest: who can put together the best Christmas stocking for the other? Thus, we stride out in search of a local market, there to forage for appropriate (and inappropriate) gifts. As can be imagined, the hunt for ever more absurd presents for each other would quickly become a source of stern competition – and regular amusement.

Budapest is memorable for one particular reason: it provides Hicky's first ever experience in a youth hostel. How he has managed to avoid spending a single night in a youth hostel for the span of his twenty-four years is beyond me but, to my glee, I find the perfect place for him to pop his cherry.

The entrance to the Red Bus Hostel could be a symbol of the long-faded glory of the Austro-Hungarian empire: ornate heavy wooden double-doors, losing their varnish, covered in graffiti and hidden behind long-abandoned scaffolding poles. Once rather grand, now very much the wrong end of shabby and we walk past it three times while looking for the entrance, discounting it as a possible option. The internal courtyard is hardly more auspicious. There's a bright blue portaloo standing in the middle.

Fortunately the hostel itself proves a little more accommodating. All the same, Hicky's verdict is rather imperious: 'Disgusting,' he declares. Personally, I think it could be worse. Hicky refuses to stay in the dormitory, so we do at least have a room and shower to ourselves.

We foray into the city and settle on dinner in the Sports Bar where we get chatting to a couple of middle-aged Englishmen. They are investment bankers with Citigroup and in Budapest on a business trip. After hearing what we are doing, they quickly return the conversation to themselves, regaling us with how great their jobs are.

The first, immediately after informing us he has a wife and two children, tells us he has the best job in the world. Travelling Europe with a girlfriend in every city. 'Home to London at the weekend to large it up!'

'Yeah,' sniggers his friend. 'Most weekdays we're working on billion-dollar deals by day and banging whores by night. It's the dream.'

It all sounds a bit desperate to be honest. 'If that's the dream, thank goodness I quit my job,' I think to myself as they sit there getting more and more drunk. Nope.

The remote life of the management consultant, away from friends and family five nights a week, is definitely not for me.

As we stroll home, Hicky and I agree that this chance encounter has reinforced our conviction that we're in the right place, doing the right thing.

'God, I wouldn't want to end up like that,' Hicky says, dragging enthusiastically on his last rollie of the night.

Budapest seems like a turning point. It feels like the west comes to an end here and something new is beginning.

TWO

Beyond the Nest

Hicky

After that, and with the dreaded portaloo indelibly printed in my mind, we resolve that from now on we should stick to passing the nights out in the rarefied airs of countryside camping spots, rather than hazarding the dubious hospitality of any more one-star hotels. Netty is becoming more than a Land Rover Defender. To us, she is a home, albeit a cramped one.

We are motoring into wine country. The great Hungarian plain that lies east of Budapest reminds us of nothing so much as the Fens in west Norfolk, not far from both our homes. Flat, green, marshy... A little dull, if I'm honest. However, the landscape begins to fold up into the Bükk Mountains just beyond our stopover for the night: the little medieval town of Eger, home to the infamous Bull's Blood blend of red wine. Legend has it that the name dates from the 16th century, when Eger Castle came under siege during the invasion of Suleiman the Magnificent in 1552. The defending Hungarians fortified themselves with plenty of local red wine. It was rumoured amongst the besieging Turks that the wine was mixed with bull's blood. How else to explain the besieged soldiers' strength and obstinate resistance? In the end, the Turks gave up, but the legend endured.

More prosaically, the earliest record of the actual wine, *Egri Bikavér* – 'Bull's Blood of Eger' – goes back only to 1912, describing it as a blend of grapes, using blue franc, Cabernet and Merlot. In actuality (and our opinion) it is just raspberry-coloured horse piss. Whatever the truth, the story does at least seem to add something to the flavour.

Eger also boasts a number of thermal baths, discovered, so we understood, by some locals prospecting for oil. We did chuckle about the look on their faces when that happened. The medicinal benefits of the baths are now at least as much of a tourist draw as the wine. Of course, we have to give one a go and end up smelling like a fishmonger's hairnet for the rest of the day.

Maintaining the wine theme, the following day we move on from Eger to the smaller town of Tokaj. Perhaps more people have heard of Tokaj's world-famous dessert wine than Eger's Bull's Blood. Indeed, Tokaj has now become a tourist trap where our intrepid Chinese friends surfaced yet again! So with prices hiked in accordance, wine tasting was going to be expensive. King Louis XV of France once described Tokaj wine to Madame de Pompadour as 'the wine of kings and the king of wines'. He was a bit of a trendsetter that Louis.

Tom and I joke that its sweet flavour seems to have rubbed off on its inhabitants whom we find a lot more charming than the folk we encountered in Eger.

Tokaj is a sweet place, generally – an attractive medieval town, situated in a loop of the Tisza River. The town and over 11,000 hectares of land around it, mostly planted with classified vineyards, was named a World Heritage Site in 2002. Naturally, we visit a vineyard to try some. The Norfolk charm must be working because the slightly saggy lass hosting our tasting can't stop laughing whenever either of us opens our mouth. At one point, she disappears out of the room, only to reappear moments later with a small vessel containing what she calls 'the Essence'.

'You very lucky,' she says. 'I give you glass for free.'

It is delicious, certainly. Like mainlining sugar, but in a good way.

She explains this stuff is very special; it is made from only the sweetest grapes and only in years when the conditions are just right. The vintage we are tasting is 1999. Even so, across the whole region, they get only twenty bottles or so of this each year. This is one of the most exclusive wines in the world, although 'technically' it cannot even be classed as a wine since its enormous sugar concentration keeps its alcohol level below about five or six per cent. On the other hand, the high sugar content means it will maintain its drinkability for over two hundred years.

'How much for a bottle?' asks Tom, taking a sip.

'Something of around eight hundred euros.'

He nearly chokes.

Suddenly the tumbler of liquid she has poured out seems a lot more generous than I had rather huffily thought before.

We spend the evening sitting on the edge of a pontoon that juts out over the smooth waters of the Tisza, swinging our legs like kids, chatting, slowly making our way through a couple more bottles of the local vintage as we watch the sun go down. They say that Norfolk has the best sunsets but already after week 1 we are witnessing skies worthy of a Constable painting. And afterwards, though the path to our beds is wending to say the least, I get the sneaking sense that we are beginning to find our feet.

Tom

It's taken a few days, but we are now heading into something that feels completely new. Unknown territory, at least for us. We squeeze up into the far north-eastern corner of Hungary and cross over into Romania, showing our passports for the first time since leaving the UK. This is our ninth international border crossing.

We get a hint that this is going to be a land of contrasts when one of the first things we see is a horse and cart being overtaken on the main road by a 1992 Mercedes SL.

That first afternoon, we are not exactly sure of our route. Having purchased a Romanian map in Hungary (bad idea by the way), we take a wrong turn in the little border town of Baia Mare and find ourselves climbing up and up, heading north towards the border with Ukraine (and the EU frontier). By now, we are already resolved on one of our 'policies': we don't go back.

Sticking to our route, we continue onwards as the road goes from asphalt to unpaved to mud track, the going becoming ever rougher. Once again, I take over from Hicky. The road cuts deeper into the hillside, gouging out a great trench in the earth, making a three-point turn impossible even if we wanted to. We either keep on, or else reverse all the way back down the mountain. The light is fading and we urgently need somewhere to make camp while we can still see. Once again, I get the jittery feeling of trepidation – that taut sensation of stretching beyond our comfort zone into the unknown. The stabilisers are slowly working themselves loose.

We almost miss it but there is suddenly a small opening in the foliage on our right-hand side. Taking it, we pass through a hedge and find ourselves in a meadow forming a wide and open lookout from the peak of the Maramureş (the small mountain range we are scaling) with a plunging view over miles and miles of ridge-lines that fall down to a plain and then climb away again into the dusk to the north, into Ukraine.

'Wow,' says Hicky.

Wow indeed.

We start pitching camp in the meadow, but almost immediately we hear the noise of a bell ringing. Some sort of herding bell. All of sudden sheep start appearing from the treeline at the back of the meadow and are shortly followed by a shepherd, presumably taking his flock off the mountain for the night. He is swarthy, with deep-set eyes, wearing a sheepskin jacket, and carrying a crook. Every inch the shepherd from a fairy-tale. We use our picture book. (This is our primary means of communication now since we don't have another language between us.) We are trying to ask the shepherd whether it's OK to camp in his field. He nods when he understands and, to be honest, looks completely uninterested by whatever the hell we want to do. It suddenly occurs to me that it's probably not his field and he was doubtless wondering why these strange foreigners were even bothering to ask.

All this may seem straightforward enough to any reader. We've driven up a mountain, found a field and made camp. Big deal. But there is something so exhilarating about this experience that it's almost transporting. It's hard to explain. Perhaps it is the uncertainty, the blood-buzz of fear, of not knowing, and then the beauty of the place, the dusk light settling softly over it all. It feels like the first taste of what lies further down our road. A taste of freedom, of adventure, as sweet as any wine.

Whatever it is, I feel so happy.

Hicky

The rest of Romania opens into another world, parts of which seem to take us back in time to a pastoral idyll, often more evocative of 16th-century England than 21st-century Europe. It's a land full of contrasts, as Tom says, from the modern to the medieval. We have arrived at the perfect time of year. Autumn is in full blaze. The hills and valleys are swathed in woodlands that dazzle with their gold, bronze and copper, red and orange, yellow and brown and fading green foliage. To say the colours are vibrant is a towering understatement. We are treated to autumn on the turn in all its glory, a sight that puts anything I've ever witnessed in England into the shade.

It all feels like a backwater, tucked away in a hidden corner of Europe, but the local Romanians are friendly, their faces often wizened and weathered. We spend the next few days zig-zagging south through the Saxon lands, as they are called, the highlight being the village of Budeşti, where a charming wooden church is encircled by massive pines, beautifully simple yet deeply evocative.

By now we have quite a well-worked camping routine. We wake at 7:28am. Emerge from the tent fifteen minutes later for a 'shower' – either under a bucket or the pathetic drip from our solar shower. (Not a product we can endorse, sadly.) Tom puts the brew on, usually in grime-encrusted mugs, while I tear off the wrapper of a long-life croissant, far past its sell-by date. Once everything is cleared away, we are usually on the road by 8:00am, having given the engine and Netty the once over. I seem to have taken that job. I'm not 100% sure what I'm looking for, true, but I just check that nothing glaringly obvious has come awry and that the engine has plenty of oil, given our 'little problem'.

In this case, it turns out none of the oil readings are correct but I quickly put this down to the fact that Netty is on a slight gradient and give her a pass. Next comes the tyre pressures which I check, only to realise that neither of us has the first clue what the correct pressure should be. Pass. One piece of technical good news, I can confirm: we have plenty of washer fluid for the windscreen.

As we make our way south, we take our time, stopping now and then at any likely-looking historical site to stretch our legs and take in the culture – notably the wooden churches of this region – and maybe even learn something. In a little place called Vatra Dornei, Tom suggests we walk up to a waterfall he's spotted. I am recovering from reconstructive knee surgery and am a bit reluctant, but he bullies me into it. It's all uphill and the rollies and nine months without exercise hasn't exactly done wonders for my fitness. It's fair to say I struggle. A black dog appears from somewhere. It's enormously fat and slow-footed. Much to Tom's amusement, the creature shuffles along at my heels all the way up to the waterfall, even stopping to wait when I need a breather.

'I feel your pain, my fat friend,' Tom wheezes, voicing what he imagines the dog must be thinking. 'I feel your pain.'

'You know it's bad form to laugh at your own jokes?' I say grumpily.

It's November now and the nights are getting a lot colder.

We are both regretting our decision in the camping shop on the Strand to go for the intermediate grade sleeping bag. I suppose we knew we would be experiencing both hot and cold climates, but the faint prospect of one day being too warm seems way too remote to bring any comfort in the middle of these autumnal nights, when even wearing more or less everything I've brought with me, I am still freezing cold. Coming from a drafty old house in Norfolk that is saying something. Fortunately we have some warmer hospitality coming.

Tom

Through his father, Hicky has managed, rather improbably, to line up another contact in this remote corner of *Mitteleuropa*. This proves to be a Hungarian nobleman called Count Tibor Kálnoky who resides in some splendour in the little town of Sighişoara, which lies about 70 miles north-west of the city of Braşov. Not far from his own impressive house, he has built a handful of guest houses where we are put up. These are pretty little cottages, architecturally very much of a piece with the traditional rural houses with which we are now well familiar. We find our lodgings very comfortable, enjoying our first proper bath since the thermal spas of Eger. (If you can call dunking ourselves in evil-smelling water 'bathing'.)

He has some other guests staying: two English journalists, both women, who are in Sighişoara to report on the several conservation projects with which the Count occupies his time. The Count himself is immaculate. A tall man in his mid-forties, who stands ramrod-straight in beautifully tailored clothes. His conversation is as immaculate as his dress, and his evident pride and love for his country and landscape breezily infectious. He entertains us for the night, introducing us to his wine cellar and generously sharing some of its contents with us and the two journalists. The next day he takes us for a walk in one of his woods. In the sprawling woodland of beech, oak and alder the colours are breathtaking. The more he talks about his country and his plans to revive it to some sort of glory, the more we fall under his spell. And the spell endures. We still agree that this part of Romania was one of the standout regions of our entire trip.

Leaving the Count's bountiful generosity behind us, we motor on down to Braşov where, naturally enough, we follow the tourist trail to Bran Castle for a day. This former Austro-Hungarian imperial hunting lodge is the inspiration – at least by way of location – for Bram Stoker's classic Gothic novel, *Dracula*. The dozens and dozens of kiosks on the approach to the castle, selling all kinds of tourist tat from bottles of 'Dracula's Blood' red wine to novelty capes, rather detract from the castle's brooding atmosphere.

Our visit to the Horezu monastery, nestled up in the Carpathian mountains about an hour west of Piteşti, leaves a more lasting impression. This complex is recognised by UNESCO as a World Heritage Site and represents the apogee of a unique architectural style known as the Brâncovenesc style. So named after a 17th-century Romanian ruler called Constantin Brâncoveanu, Prince of Wallachia, who was a great patron of culture. He had particular influence over architectural design, mural and sculptural painting, and other forms of religious art, combining the Neo-Byzantine style with the more innovative ideas of the Italian Renaissance. He intended the Horezu monastery to serve as his tomb. In fact, he wasn't buried there, but his death was nevertheless remarkable. He was a vassal ruler to the Ottoman Turks who, in 1714, still held sovereignty over the princedom of Wallachia, and on the occasion of his 60th birthday he was summoned before the Sultan at the time to Istanbul. Whereupon the Sultan confiscated all his worldly goods and ordered him to renounce his faith in submission to Islam, along with his four sons. He refused, standing firm in his Christian faith, and so he and all his sons were duly executed – all of them beheaded and their bodies and heads then thrown into the waters of the Bosporus. After this rather grisly episode, Brâncoveanu was soon canonised in the Romanian Orthodox faith.

Perhaps the spirit of this old saint haunts the quiet basilicas and colonnades of Horezu yet. Neither of us is particularly spiritual, but we are both still touched by the serenity of the place. Rubber-necking our way around the complex, we inadvertently invade the main church whilst a service is in play, feeling like a couple of unwashed barbarians.

Gesturing to the sisters we encounter near the door, they signal that we are welcome to come inside and join the service. At first we stand at the back admiring the spectacular murals that cover the walls. But then we are ushered forward to a point about mid-way down the nave. From there we watch and take in the Gregorian chant rising up into the hollow cupolas above our heads, the murmured prayers echoing off the walls and the liturgies rippling off the lips of the gathered monks and nuns in the congregation. It isn't long before I feel entirely capti-vated by the spiritual power of the place. By a presence I sense, in fact. I find myself being deeply affected by this, and a glance at Hicky's face tells me that he is feeling something similar. Afterwards outside we agree it is the best thing we have yet experienced on the trip, probably our most moving spiritual experience ever. It stays with us a long time.

Hicky
From the lofty spiritual and cultural heights of Transylvania, we now descend to the eastern lowlands of Romania, picking up the motorway at Piteşti and bypassing the capital, Bucharest, in our rush to reach the inland waterways. We then head north and east, dropping down to sea level into what is now the delta of the mighty Danube.

For the second time, we are reminded of home. This is the largest inland water system in Europe, but again looks like nothing so much as the Norfolk Broads. After the golden glories of the Carpathian mountains in all their autumnal garb, the flat marshland and the thin line of the horizon dampens the spirits some. (Although we realise we should get used to that, knowing what lies ahead.)

Our campsite for the night is as damp and muddy as you would expect in the Fens, too. Aside from our brief sojourn as guests of Count Tibor, we have been camping for five nights on the trot so showering and washing our clothes has been difficult to say the least. Many methods have been tried on the personal hygiene front including Tom's approach of just filling a bowl with water, adding soap and pouring it over his head. My method involves the same bowl of water but is somewhat daintier: I just put my feet in and scrub away with a washing-up cloth. This usually occurs on a hill and in full view of various Romanian homesteads; quite what they thought when they saw two very white, skinny, naked and badly bearded English gentlemen trying these various techniques is not known.

As for our cooking – after a barren breakfast consisting of a piece of mouldy fruit and that foil-wrapped croissant, followed by a game of luncheon lottery at a very local village restaurant, we are both starving by early evening. Neither of us are renowned for our culinary skills back in England but, armed with tins of various varieties, packets of assorted carbohydrates and more gas than the Ukraine, we set to work. By now, this being the third week away from home, we have become sterling field chefs with a vast array of cooking talent, which still relates entirely and only to beans and dried sausages. There follows a typical recipe:

- 1 x tin of tomatoes
- 1 x tin of kidney beans
- 1 x tin of white beans
- 1 x tin of beans unknown
- 1 x finely chopped local sausage
- A dash of local red wine
- A very large pinch of salt
- An even larger pinch of dried chilli

Method: put everything into a pan and simmer for fifteen minutes. Serve with a plastic cup of local red wine.

It is a miserable night, the rain never letting up for a second. Come morning, it is still raining. We decide to wait to see if a break will come, reluctant to get soaked first thing and probably remain soaked all day. After an hour or so, there is a lull in the downpour and we pack everything up in a rush and get on the road. A piece of luck, since it then continues to rain for the rest of the day.

However, I am afraid this is one of my weaker performances on the map. Shortly after our departure, our route becomes a little confused. An hour of driving later, we pass our campsite of the night before.

'Oh well. I'm sure you'll get us there in the end,' says Tom, rather unhelpfully.

The final stopover on our way out of Romania is the small city of Tulcea, set in the very heart of the Danubian delta, about twenty miles from the Black Sea proper. Remarkably, this place dates all the way back to the 7th-century BC, beginning life as a Greek trading colony (as did a lot of the cities dotted around the Black Sea). It has since come under the sway of, variously, the Romans, the Byzantines and the Turks as each age of empire came and went. Even the Central Powers held it for a couple of years during the Great War before it came back into Romanian hands.

But these days, if it's renowned for anything, it is as a haunt for twitchers. The Danube delta is one of the best places in the world for bird watching. (Putting even our own Norfolk Broads in the shade.)

We arrive out of season. November is a drab month down there, even with the sun shining. The shuttered shops, hostelries and restaurants, and the deserted pontoons and quays, all give the impression that the townsfolk are marking time, sitting out the winter until the tourists begin arriving again, presumably in the spring. They have a long wait ahead.

But Tom and I have some business for one boatman, at least.

After much bartering in various forms of pidgin to many of the local boatmen, we select a skipper named 'Phil'. That's what Tom calls him anyway – the first of many other 'Phils' whom we shall meet down the road. (I believe his actual name is Vasily.) Skipper Phil has a red-moon face with thick spectacles slung askew across his nose. His square-set body bulges out of a faded green jacket. Despite the language barrier, he seems a jolly fellow. He would have us believe that his boat is a mighty vessel with speeds of up to eight knots.

The following morning, suffering two sizeable hangovers from an evening sinking some kind of highly flammable local spirit, we are ready. Just about. We throw off the painter and drift away from the quayside. It all starts simply enough, the experienced boatman showing us around the waterways and pointing out various lakes and bird colonies while, according to Tom, I bark at the Captain about the joys of the Norfolk Broads and the Golden Plover. All of a sudden we both find ourselves holding a shot glass full of Tuica: Skipper Phil's home-made vodka. Or perhaps it was wine. Or maybe a kind of schnapps. Whatever it is supposed to be, it is reddish and tastes of plums. It's ten o'clock in the morning, but we knock it back. Rude not to, I suppose.

It burns like fire.

Tom wonders aloud whether this stuff powers the motor as well. Skipper Phil just grins at us.

The trip is supposed to take four hours, which – we imagine – will allow us to cover quite an area and hopefully see some interesting wildlife. Unfortunately we quickly realise that Skipper Phil's vessel has a top speed of something around walking pace (what was all that eight knot talk?) so we decide to lower our expectations, settling ourselves in to enjoy the sun, the water and the trees, sharpened by the occasional chaser of rocket-fuel. When Skipper Phil produces another bottle – this one containing an even more suspicious liquor syphoned into a crumpled Coca-Cola bottle and smelling of urine, Tom at least is game to try it. He finds a picture of an apple in The Book and compliments Skipper Phil on his cider. Phil is mortified. 'Vino,' he protests.

If that's wine, we really have come to the end of the road here, in more ways than one.

Perhaps no thanks to our alcoholic helmsman, we do actually spot an eagle. Apparently a rare sighting. Using The Book and a lot of patience, Tom discovers that in 1990 there were only eight nesting pairs in the whole delta and even today there are only twenty-five to thirty. Meanwhile I am barking at Skipper Phil about the joys of witnessing the screams of a mating pair of Golden Plover first hand. (The jet-fuel must be taking effect.)

'You're not bad with that thing, are you?' I say at our slap-up feast that night – meaning The Book. We are celebrating our last night in Romania with a three-course meal, a bottle of Tuica (not home-made) and several other bottles of Romanian wine.

'It's that or sit there like a pair of mutes from now on.'

Ironically, this is exactly the state to which we are reduced by the end of the night. In the final bar before our beds, we sit in silence like a pair of anacondas, slowly digesting a bellyful of Romanian stodge, our heads befuddled with booze. Not exactly the recipe for a bright start the next morning, when we say goodbye to Europe and hello to the ghost-lands of the Soviet Union.

THREE

The East Begins

Tom

From Tulcea, it's a drive of about 65 miles to the Moldovan border. Driving north, we understand that, from now on, things are going to be a bit different.

The countryside is unremarkable. The Danube delta rises into hillier country as we approach Moldova. The roads are lined with walnut trees and behind them, sunflower fields – a long way off next summer's flowering – or newly planted wheat fields and the occasional vineyard.

Our plan is to drive some way to the north of the Moldovan capital, Chișinău, to visit the cave monasteries at Orhei. These were dug out of the cliffs by monks in the 13th century, and have been occupied continually ever since. The day we visit only the main chapel is open. We climb up to it and are delighted to find a couple getting married. Then less delighted when we learn that the monastery hotel – affording five rooms overlooking the cliffs – is closed.

We drive back down into Chișinău and look for an alternative. It is late in the day so we try the first place we come across, ignoring the gaudy neon lights and somewhat seedy veneer.

'How many hours you want room?' asks the receptionist from behind hooded eyelids. 'We have double available for next three hour.'

We exchange a dubious look.

'You know what?' says Hicky determinedly. 'I think we'll keep looking.'

We beat a hasty retreat, eventually finding somewhere that passes Hicky's exacting standards. At sixty dollars a night, we reckon they've done pretty well out of us, but it's a good place to sleep off the previous night's excesses.

The next day, rather than heading direct for Odessa, over the Ukrainian border, we decide we are going to have a stab at getting into the tiny state of Transnistria.

Transnistria is a break-away republic within a break-away republic, reminiscent of Churchill's description of Russia: 'a riddle, wrapped in a mystery, inside an enigma'. Supplied with arms and ammunition by Russia it declared its independence in 1990. After a brief scrap in 1992 it would appear the Moldovan government opted for the path of least resistance and allowed them simply to get on with it. As a result, Transnistria now has its own currency (not recognised outside its own borders), parliament, president and borders. However, as a nation it is not recognised by a single member of the United Nations and so a Transnistrian passport is about as much use as a chocolate teapot. We have read that it is a last bastion of true Soviet communism, very much Russian-facing (as opposed to the west) and an altogether unwelcoming place for western foreigners. Our guidebook and the FCO website are unequivocal in their advice that it is not somewhere to visit unless you have a pressing need.

Of course, this is a red rag to our 4x4 bull.

Still, our hubris only carries us so far and the closer we get to the border, the more nervous we both become. The realisation that neither of us has ever had to square up to any sort of tough border crossing suddenly hits us rather starkly.

'Are you sure we've got the right documentation?' Hicky says for the third time.

'I guess we're about to find out.'

We are on what we have decided is the main road through Transnistria, and getting close to the Dnister River now. With my head buried in the map, I suddenly feel the car round a bend and then hear Hicky muttering, 'Wiendish, wiendish, wiendish!' [Translation: *This is some serious shit*.] Naturally I look up... and am confronted with a tank, a machine gun nest and several soldiers armed with automatic weapons.

Hicky's turn of phrase is extremely unhelpful as it triggers in me a fit of nervous giggles that would shame a schoolgirl and which I can't control even as he is bringing Netty to a halt beside two angry-looking soldiers.

Hicky

The first thing they ask us is if we are carrying any guns or narcotics. Fortunately, we both realise this probably isn't the time for jokes. I resolve not to mention my spud gun in the back. They soon cotton on to what we, in fact, are: overlanders.

To them, this means free stuff.

Now ordinarily at this point, I would hop out and joke and laugh and slap a back or two and maybe share a cigarette, while Tom opens up the back of Netty like an East End barrow boy laying out his stall of English souvenirs. ('Nice box of PG Tips for you, sir? 'n I'll throw in a luv-verly photograph of 'er Maj as well?') However, in this case, I don't feel back-slapping is the answer. Instead, in a panic, I find myself offering the nearest guard my Norfolk tweed flat cap – a prized possession, the loss of which I would mourn deeply. The guard takes it, turns it over, then gestures that it's good for nothing but wiping his arse. (No taste, these Moldovans ... although I am secretly very glad to get it back.)

Meanwhile Tom is rather sheepishly offering the guard's mate a jar of our beloved Nescafé Gold Blend – coffee which far outshines anything we've come across in these parts. This, apparently, is sufficient payment as they then inform us we have missed the border and are in the process of attempting an illegal border crossing. They redirect us, we find the correct road, and I continue driving until the 'Stop' sign, pulling over as directed. The guard waves me out of the vehicle, then walks me back up the road thirty yards to a sign reading 'Police' and, in hatchet English, explains that I should have stopped there instead. Result: a spot fine of thirty dollars cash. No receipt.

Only then are we told that this border crossing is for locals only and that foreigners need to use another one some distance back. Eventually we find the right crossing. I unclip my seatbelt as we come to a halt in preparation for getting out and showing our papers. This, I'm told, is a fine-able offence. Twenty dollars cash this time. No receipt. By now, I'm beginning to feel like the new boy at prep school who keeps having his trousers pulled down and all his sweets taken off him. Nor am I feeling alto-gether well-disposed towards the Moldovan military.

The Transnistrians are little better. We show the guards

our passports, freshly stamped from Moldova, but one of them complains that we have only 'Entry' stamps and no 'Exit' stamps. We offer to go back to get the correct stamp, although Tom is sceptical that any such stamp even exists – and given that the Moldovans don't view entry into Transnistria as 'leaving' he is probably right. In any case, the guard refuses, instead demanding another thirty greenbacks. No receipt.

Finally we have made it through to Transnistrian immigration. We progress, thanks to a lovely man on the desk, who charges us only fifteen dollars, and even provides us with a receipt! This brings our total expenditure to $125 for the privilege of entering this strange little non-country.

So what do we find? Is it worth the trouble and expense? I think it isn't. Tom thinks it definitely is.

It's a short drive from the border into the capital of Tiraspol. We notice that a lot of shops, gas stations and other outlets are branded with the name 'Sheriff' – apparently the only company in the country. We later learn that the owners of this company drive around the place in a fleet of ten black Humvees with blacked-out windows, while the rest of the population have to make do on a national GDP per capita of $1,500 per annum. Communism at its best.

As we enter the city we spot our first statue of Comrade Lenin, looking stern and imperious as ever.

Tom is drinking it all in. 'It's exactly as I imagined it to be,' he says, although I have to wonder why a man would spend any time at all imagining the capital of Transnistria. Apparently he is impressed with an austere-looking tank perched on a pedestal and flying the 'national' flag.

It certainly is grim. Severe, sharp-edged government

buildings with forbidding frontages; elsewhere row upon row of grey and rather shabby residential tower blocks. The city centre is cut through with wide boulevards that are more concrete than trees. Occasionally the golden cupolas of a white-washed church break the drabness, gleaming dully in the afternoon light.

Soon after the tank, we are pulled over at a checkpoint and asked once more whether we have narcotics or guns on board. This time we do laugh and soon we are exchanging cigarettes instead. Tom pushes his luck and asks whether he can get a photo of the famous tank. (Every piece of advice we have read says the fastest way to get arrested in Transnistria is to take photographs in public.) This soldier doesn't seem bothered so Tom runs back and is delighted to get his shot, chalking this up as a kind of victory after the border-entry shake-down.

Leaving Transnistria is not a lot easier than entering it, although we have become a little wiser. After a considerable amount of inventive chat – mainly bigging up our expedition, our reportage on what we have seen, and our non-existent celebrity status back in England – we manage to haggle the exit fee down from $200 to $40. I am very happy to pay $200 if it means leaving this strange little non-country behind us.

Tom
The less said about Hicky's border negotiations, the better. If I'm not nearby to keep an eye on proceedings, he'll happily take the first number anyone gives him – and then add a tip. Still, we are through. Onwards to the Ukraine! Immediately, it is different. The border guards, although hidden behind flu masks, are the soul of charm compared with the Moldovans and Transnistrians.

We are soon speeding through the flatlands towards our destination for the day, the Black Sea port of Odessa. At the city limits, we get lost. We stop at a shop to ask the way to our hotel. The couple inside are so helpful that they pursue us down the street in their enthusiasm to set us on the right road. This is a taste of things to come.

The city of Odessa was an 18th-century creation of Prince Potemkin, the Russian Empress Katerina's favourite lover. As a port city, it has always been a cosmopolitan place, reflected by the make-up of its population. At the turn of the 20th century, the census shows a healthy mixture of Russians, Jews, Ukrainians, Germans, Poles, Greeks, Tatars, Armenians, Belarusians and even Frenchmen. These days, after the convulsions of two World Wars, the Jewish population is still present, but vastly reduced in number and the Frenchmen seem to have been replaced with Bulgarians. Despite that, the city has retained its cosmopolitan feel. The Italian influence in the architecture is obvious – with beautiful classical-style buildings lining leafy boulevards, giving it a pleasant and cultured atmosphere, even in early November, albeit it is very cold.

When we finally make it to our hotel in Odessa we assess the damage inflicted on our wallets by the Transnistrian 'police force' and head out to find a cheap local restaurant for dinner. This results in a menu of vodka, pig fat, borsch, and for pudding ... chocolate and bacon. After this questionable feast we are able to get some well-earned rest.

The next day we take a look around the city. At the Pivoz market we do another round of stocking-filler shopping. Two pairs of novelty boxer shorts and, more practically for the journey ahead, a piece of string and a thermometer. A successful excursion, by our reckoning. Preparation for a long drive tomorrow.

It's around 450 miles from Odessa to the Russian border – more or less due east. With all our clothes now freshly washed, a full tank of fuel and stocked up on food, we drive through the day, snacking our lunch at the wheel. We realise we have entered new topography – the south-western rim of the great Ukrainian steppe. The road cutting through it is arrow-straight. There is nothing to look at, just endless horizon beyond fields with no hedges. Despite the monotony of the landscape and the long hours in the cab, one never feels bored. A baseline level of adrenaline hums along in the blood with the sound of the engine as the miles clock up and whatever lies just beyond the horizon creeps ever closer.

By the time darkness is falling we are surprised to have covered only around 300 miles, reaching a short distance beyond a city called Melitopol. The only feature in the landscape is a thin strip of woodland, so we pull off and drive down the track beside it. We notice a tractor and wonder whether the farmer might move us along, but he doesn't seem to care. He leaves us to set up camp in peace. By now it is spitting sleet and the mercury has fallen well below zero.

The idea of preparing supper and eating outside is hideously unappealing so we relocate to the back of Netty for the first time. This works well. We manage to stay warm while the sleet lashes at the windows, although the prospect of sleeping 'upstairs' in the tent as the temperature continues to drop is far from enticing.

The wind picks up during the night, putting our roof-tent through its paces. By morning, the temperature has risen back above freezing which is no help at all. Sleet turns to rain; frozen hard ground turns to thick mud and covers everything as we dismantle our camp. By the time we climb into the cab, I'm soaked through and filthy. For the remaining distance to the Russian border, Hicky takes the wheel while I sit huddled against the heater, drying myself out in small patches at a time. It is, thus, in a miserable state that we now enter the Motherland.

Hicky

We're over the Russian border with relative ease. No fines, at least. However, at the first road-block thirty miles further on, we are fined a hundred US dollars for not having the correct insurance. We debate whether this is a genuine thing, but the point is moot since we are led – like lambs to the slaughter – to an office where we are sold the correct insurance for the further *modest* sum of eighty US dollars. Tom's journal records that the policeman was extremely friendly and even took him personally to the right place to get the insurance. As well he might. The kindest shake-down in southern Russia.

Our wallets a little lighter, we push on towards Rostov-na-Donu through the driving rain which has not let up for a single minute all day. We find another camping spot, fairly similar to the night before only this time, after cowering in the back of Netty and eating a hastily cooked stew, when we head 'upstairs' we discover that the zip to the roof-tent flap is frozen solid.

This leaves us in a rather unpleasant quandary until I come up with my now trademarked technique of 'suck-and-spit'. Inch by dogged inch, I finally succeed in loosening the zip and we tumble inside for the night, dragging half a field of mud in with us covering everything – which makes the night especially unpleasant.

'Look at it this way,' I say, trying to put a brave face on it. 'If we survive tonight, then we're on to Stalingrad tomorrow.'

'Oh joy,' Tom replies with that sardonic look of his.

We are learning that while Tom may be more adventurous on the road, I am more willing to roll up my sleeves and get on with the more unpleasant challenges of the 'overlander's life'.

By the time we roll into Volgograd (as the city of Stalingrad is now known), there are suspicious rumblings in my belly. Through judicious use of the BlackBerry translator and quite a lot of begging, we manage to persuade a hotel clerk to let us take a room in his establishment for a couple of nights, despite the fact that we have no confirmed reservation in his hotel on our visa entry form. While this back and forth continues, my physical condition goes south fast. As I later wrote in my journal, 'Horrendous bowel and flu-like symptoms hit me like a heavyweight punch in the guts for the next twenty-four hours.' We identify the culprit as the sausage that we had flung – rather carelessly, it turned out – into our stew on the road. It was certainly of indeterminate age, its provenance probably Romania, although possibly as far back as the Somme.

I lie whaling around in my bed – between hasty visits to the bathroom – while Tom goes off to find an internet cafe where he hopes to set up a Skype account so he can more easily talk with home. I detect in him the merest hint of gloating that he has avoided my self-administered food-poisoning. However, it is not long before he returns to the room, looking decidedly grey of gill and complaining of unholy stirrings within.

So there we both lie for the rest of the day.

'What followed was a truly horrific night,' writes Tom in his journal.

I can only reflect that even a low-grade Russian hotel room is a preferable place to endure a twenty-four-hour stomach meltdown to rival Chernobyl, than in a canvas tent out on the steppe. Thanks to the loud Russian house music blaring from the dance-floor of a wedding nearby, we are spared the worst of the noises emanating from the bathroom as we each take our turn. So virulent is the attack that we work our way through several rolls of toilet paper. Every time we run out, one of us has to take the empty roll and wave it at the night clerk at reception. An obliging chap, he must have replaced our supply at least four times.

The following day, we scrape ourselves out of our room for a couple of hours around lunchtime, do a little prep on the journey ahead in the internet cafe, only to scurry back to our ever-more squalid little burrow.

The day after we begin to feel more normal. It is Remembrance Sunday back home in England – an appropriate day for remembering the war dead, and there are surely enough to recall in and around this city.

Any history of the Second World War will tell you that the Battle of Stalingrad was a turning point in the fate of Nazi Germany and the outcome of the war. It raged from late August 1942 through to the beginning of February 1943 when the beleaguered German 6th Army at last surrendered. Stalingrad was, of course, a decisive Soviet victory, albeit at the cost of well over a million military casualties. The civilian casualties were unimaginably high, too – under Stalin's orders, none had been allowed to evacuate the city. The accurate figure is unknown because the Soviets stopped recording civilian casualties early on in the five-month battle.

The bloodiest battle of the war, the Soviets have chosen to commemorate their victory in truly epic style. A colossal statue entitled *The Motherland Calls* rises from the western bank of the Volga River on the Mamayev Kurgan to a height of eighty-five metres. It depicts a woman – allegorical of the Motherland – with a sword pointing in defiance against the west (or Germany, in particular). It is quite awesome to behold. And the memorial complex at its feet is the most dramatic and impressive that either of us have ever visited, even though the text is in Russian and unintelligible to us. The ceiling to floor circular walls inscribed with hundreds of thousands of names is particularly sobering.

Aside from the shadow of these epic events looming so large over this city, we decide we quite like Volgograd. By Sunday our bowels are feeling human again. So, on Monday morning we pack up and steel ourselves for the road ahead, and what will be perhaps the strangest section of our entire journey.

FOUR

———

Wilderness

Tom

We know that from Volgograd to the Kazakh port of Aktau we have about five days in the tent ahead of us – likely in the freezing cold under a desert moon. Even so, we set out in good spirits with all the levity of men making good their escape from an unpleasant illness. We sweep south along the western bank of the Volga, ditching the main road to trundle along its sandy banks and admire its blue waters, the flat brown landscape beyond and the chasm of clear sky above. I am driving, feeling free and optimistic about the road ahead.

Perhaps a little too free. Around lunchtime, we are pulled over by the police. I suspect another shake-down.

Hicky

The police take Tom away, put him in the back of their van and climb in after him. Disconcerted, I am left to kick the tyres and nervously puff my way through a couple of cigarettes. A man pops up – from where I still have no idea – but he can speak perfect English. He's not a cop so I deduce that he MUST be a member of the KGB.

'What's the problem?' he said, taking the cigarette I'm offering him.

'I don't know. They've got my friend in their van over there.'

'Is he in trouble?'

I suspect at least our wallets are in trouble. I shrug. 'You tell me. He's been in there twenty minutes.'

'Let's take a look,' suggests my new friend.

We shuffle up to the van and peer through the back window. I am surprised to see the arresting officer convulsing with laughter.

Tom

The first thing I notice about the two officers escorting me to their van is how un-Russian they look. We are nearly at the Kazakh border and these two have classically Central Asian features: round, naturally friendly looking faces, darker skin, narrower eyes. Very different to the hard-jawed, severe features of their western colleagues.

They usher me into their van and sit me on a single chair bolted to the floor in the back of the vehicle. They take up positions on two chairs facing me. It's interview time. Before the questions begin they show me a video of Netty doing 97kph in a 60kph zone. The first two thoughts that go through my mind are strange. The first is pride: 97kph? Who knew the Netster had it in her! The second is relief: that this is a genuine misdemeanour and not just another shake-down by corrupt cops.

'Too fast. There is fine,' says one. 'Standard fine–' Don't tell me. '–One hundred dollar.'

Despite the fact that I have clearly been caught bang to rights I've heard 'one hundred dollar' once too often. I decide to take a new approach. Feigning horror and in spite of the cramped space, I stand up and start undoing my belt. 'You want a hundred dollars,' I cry. 'You want my trousers as well? Why not take them too?' By now, my belt is undone and my trousers are heading south. Sitting back down with my trousers round my knees, I spread my hands wide and give them a look that says, 'Well, do you!'

For a good few seconds the two cops are stunned to silence. But then, the initial shock passing, they collapse into gales of laughter. I flop back in the seat and start laughing myself. Moments later, we are old buddies, joking and grinning, while one of the policemen pulls out his phone and starts showing me photos of his family and, somewhat bizarrely, the legendary hardman Steven Seagal. 'The Gull,' as Hicky and I have referred to him for years, is a personal favourite of ours so, using only pidgin and sign language, I desperately try to understand the link. We chat away for some time but, despite lots of animation and effort on both sides, I am no closer to understanding the connection when there is a knock at the window. It's Hicky.

Fast forward another twenty minutes and we are exchanging gifts. We re-board Netty having acquired the badge from one of their police hats and two dried fish for our pot, in exchange for a handheld plastic Union Jack and some Tetley teabags. We drive away, watching the figure in the rear-view mirror growing smaller and smaller. He is still waving his little Union Jack as we round the bend – enough to warm even the most unpatriotic of hearts.

'Ironic, isn't it?' I say.

'What?'

'The only time we've ever genuinely done something wrong and we don't pay a fine.'

Hicky

Feeling our luck riding high, we skirt the edge of Astrakhan with barely a glance, keen instead to camp as close to the Kazakh border as possible so that we could cross at dawn the next day. This is what we do, hazarding nothing more adventurous than a can of soup on our still delicate constitutions. As anticipated, it is excruciatingly cold – though we would shortly be experiencing much colder.

At the crack of dawn the next day we load up, making sure to check everywhere underneath the chassis for stowed contraband. We reckon we provide a rather obvious target for those more unprincipled criminal elements to use us as unwitting mules for moving illicit goods across the border. The effect of doing this serves less to reassure us that there are no drugs on board than it does simply to stoke our already-high stress levels. Nevertheless, as satisfied as we can be, we drive the short distance to the border.

Just before the first checkpoint we switch seats because I'm named as the driver on the carnet for Netty. In this instance, the Kazakhs have passengers clear immigration through one channel while the driver and his vehicle progress through another. So, we are split up for a while, separated by a chain-mail fence.

It is this separation – oh, and the stoked levels of stress, and the days of broken sleep, and the bad stomachs – that cause our first real falling-out. (It shall be noted that it is also one of our *only* fall-outs of the whole trip, which always erupt out of something completely trivial.)

But first a little context.

Both of us have brought various items to serve as mementos of life back home and, I suppose, to stave off

home-sickness, should it ever rear its miserable head. Tom
has brought, amongst other things, a tennis ball – and
not just any tennis ball. It is a Queen's Club Tennis Ball.
Suffice to say, it has sentimental value, the true extent of
which I am about to find out.

While the crossing into Kazakhstan is not as tricky as
the Moldovan–Transnistrian border, it is nevertheless
laborious. The customs official – a rather corpulent
gentleman with sweat beading down his temples in spite
of the chilly air – insists that I remove just about every
single article from the back of Netty while he pores over
each item in turn. I apply my usual tactic of disarmingly
cheerful familiarity in the hope that this might expedite
the process, and it is not long before I am resorting
to offering a free memento to put the seal on our new
friendship. I am about to offer him another flag – which
worked so well last time – when his eyes alight on Tom's
precious Queen's Club Tennis Ball. He picks it up and
starts playing around with it. He seems quite taken with
it.

'Keep it,' I say, giving him my warmest grin. He doesn't
seem to understand so I press it into his hands. 'It's a gift.
From us to you.'

Suddenly a voice breaks like thunder across the
forecourt. 'Put that fucking ball down right now!' Just like
the scene from *There's Something About Mary* involving a
baseball.

I turn to see a crimson-faced Tom clawing at the chain-
mail fence like The Gull himself in a desperate moment
of dire peril. 'What the hell are you doing, Hickman?
Don't you fucking dare!'

I stand nonplussed, hackles rising, since I am only
doing my best to smooth our transition into this damned

country. The guard is staring at Tom with a look of terror and bewilderment, and seemingly in the grip of Tom's wrathful tirade, he tosses the ball back to me.

He takes the loss a little easier than Tom.

Afterwards, once everything is loaded up again, I progress through to the Kazakh side and am reunited with my – by now – extremely irate passenger. Despite my most obsequious apologies, he gives me the cold shoulder for the first hundred kilometres into Kazakhstan, playing angry hip-hop – mostly the west coast variety of Tupac, Dre and N.W.A. – until his temper has cooled.

We are still not speaking when we come across our first camel. A pair of them, in fact, wandering along beside the road. The Russian steppe has given way to proper desert now. But under the circumstances, all of this passes with no comment.

Tom

At the first (and last) petrol station we will come to for a while, the dark clouds break and I decide that, on balance, a tennis ball is a rather pointless thing to be angry about after all. Perhaps I just needed to vent some stress after worrying all morning about doing yet another border crossing. And Hicky was only doing what he thought best…

The angry hip hop goes off. Normal service is resumed with a quiet apology.

And so, with a full tank of petrol, we strike out into what would be the strangest section of our journey to date – the Qaraqalpak desert of Western Kazakhstan. The sun soars high in this land, and under it the landscape shines white and wide, seeming almost flattened by the weight of the blue abyss above.

For now the road surface remains good. We drive all afternoon seeing little in the way of habitation and making good time. For the first time we decide to push on into the night. It is rather extraordinary: we hardly need our headlamps since the starlight is so bright. When eventually we pull off the road we simply turn ninety degrees to the road and strike out into the desert. Once far enough away to be out of sight we stop and make camp. With no unnatural light for as far as the eye can see we look up and appreciate the vast canopy of the universe in all its glory. Neither of us have ever seen the like. The Milky Way stands out in a thick band of white light, stretching from one horizon to the other. We have no need of torches to set up camp, everything is lit with the stars' ethereal light – meanwhile overhead, shooting stars pop away as regularly as fireworks on Bonfire Night.

We climb into our tent and fall asleep, our hearts full with the serene solitude of the desert. However, the romantic wildness of our situation soon evaporates, along with the last of any heat residual from the daylight sun. Within a couple of hours, both of us are awake, shivering and frozen to the marrow. Never one to do things by halves, Hicky decides he won't stand for it and pulls on more or less all the clothes that he has. Two or three pairs of shooting stockings (an enduring totem of his Englishness in even the remotest corners of the world), jeans under tracksuit bottoms, two jumpers (cashmere, of course), a thick woollen hat and who knows what else. Despite all this, it is still too cold to go back to sleep. I swiftly follow suit, draping my coat over my sleeping bag as a final layer.

It is nowhere near enough. At 5 in the morning, both awake and with teeth chattering, we concede defeat and are forced to get up in search of a cup of tea and Netty's heater.

'Tea's off,' says Hicky.

'Why?' I ask.

He gives our five-litre jerry can a kick. It is frozen solid. We pack up. Never have I regretted Netty's totally ineffectual heater more (a relic from the fifties). We set off in the dark, huddled over the pathetic trickle of warm air making its way out of the heating vents. Eventually, mercifully, everything begins to heat up and we are treated to another astonishing day. We watch out of our windows as the dawn rises over the steppe, lighting up hundreds of miles of wilderness to the east first in grey, then yellow, then gold and finally, perfect sunshine. We are fairly buzzing along, circumventing the small border town of Beyneu – a glorified infrastructure depot – when all at once the asphalt surface ends, giving way to a purgatory of dust and grit. The 'road' lurches and heaves about the Netster and threatens to rattle the teeth from our jaws. Our speed drops to a crawl.

The road is so bad in fact that it has been abandoned by most who have gone before us. Tracks weave left and right, intersecting, trailing into nothing. We even pass a lorry apparently forging a new path through the desert steppe, way off to one side of us, barrelling and bumping over the thick tufts of desert scrub, kicking up a fog of dust in its wake, the cab bucking like a bronco.

We have a go at that ourselves and find it works as well as anything else. Probably not great for Netty's suspension admittedly. This is 'man vs road'. Or more precisely, machine vs road. We hope our game old lady is up to the task.

We plough on like this for a good 150km – five or

six hours of exhausting driving – before the panoramic flat desert gives way to a canyon that drops us down and down into a kind of moonscape. By this stage, we have the driving technique down to an art. The vibrations from the corrugated grit demand a sort of Goldilocks approach: the speed not too fast, not too slow. Just so... the optimum being about 20mph.

At last we climb out of the canyon and shortly beyond the upper rim we are met not only with a sensational view but also the return of the asphalt – cue high fives, a photo shoot, plenty of back stretches, and a celebratory rollie for Hicky.

We fly through the last two hundred kilometres to the Caspian port city of Aktau. After the Qaraqalpaki wastelands, rolling into town is rather surreal. New office blocks, tacky-looking restaurants with garish signs offering burgers and beer, hotels of glass and steel that glisten in the bright sunshine. We also spot our first petrol station since starting our desert run two days ago. Having driven solidly for two days, our investment in a long-range fuel tank has finally paid out in full.

We draw up at the first hotel we come to, The Grand Hotel Victory, resplendent in its shiny blue and white facade. It's probably the nicest one in town, we later discover, there to cater for the men and women who service the oil industry and its black gold. When we discover it is four hundred US dollars a night, I baulk at the idea and say we should find somewhere else.

Hicky goes white at the suggestion. 'I need this,' he begs. 'It may sound pathetic, but I really do.'

It's the third time he's pulled this card and, since I vetoed the first two, I eventually submit to his pleas.

As advertised – 1999 (S) Defender 110, 192,000 miles, great condition. 'We can offer this vehicle to you for £3,950 + VAT.' Done!

Wonderful Netty Hedges of the British Red Cross. Recovered from three strokes, taught us first aid – our vehicle was named in her honour.

Netty in action – the expedition's first off-piste camp spot. Gera Lario, Lake Como.

The startled rabbit – first-night nerves, softened by red wine and indeterminate carbs. Somme valley.

One star – Hicky's first 'hostel' experience, Budapest.

Rush hour, Maramures, N. Romania.

One of the many daily treats, opening the tent onto magical vistas.
Vatra Dornei, Romania.

Heading home – joining the horses at dusk. Viscri, Romania.

A spectacular wild camping spot. Autumnal Romania at its very best. Camping in rusty shades, Horezu, Romania.

Star 'in Grad.
Volgograd, Russia.

Inside dining – the meal that single-handedly depleted Volgograd's loo-roll supplies. North-east of Rostov-na-Donu, Russia.

International relations I – Tom going to great lengths to avoid paying a fine. Trousers back on by this point. Narimanov, Russia.

International relations II – Hicky less than impressed with his half of the trade: dried river fish. Narimanov, Russia.

Captain on deck! Hicky trying his hand on the bridge, stuck outside Baku harbour, Caspian Sea.

Ta'arof! Our first experience of Persian hospitality. Note who's wearing the Norfolk flat cap. Lavandvil, Iran.

Below: desert driving outside Atyrau, Kazakhstan.

In the Iranian mountains. Note rubbed-out border
negotiations on Netty's side. Dasht Taharom, Iran.

The Mud City – Yazd, Iran.

Hicky

It's not so much the creature comforts I need. I just like a decent bed, clean sheets without stains and a shower that isn't like a dripping tap. To be clean. Is that too much to ask for?

I refuse to feel too guilty about it, since the concierge, even without Les Clefs d'Or, proves very useful, helping us get organised for the Caspian Sea crossing from Aktau to Baku in Azerbaijan, which isn't exactly straightforward. We have heard much about this fabled ship crossing. From reports on various travel blogs we know that there is no precise schedule and that the variable weather means that the cargo crossings may grind to a halt at a moment's notice, allowing all involved a well-earned breather. For the time being then we find ourselves at the mercy of the Kazakh/Azeri shipping industry. Not exactly your P&O from Dover to Calais.

The concierge tells us to go to the port to arrange stowing Netty on the next cargo ship arriving from Baku. After much investigation at the port we eventually find an engineer called Ruslan, who would act as a sort of agent for a ride to Azerbaijan. It is Thursday morning when we meet him. He tells us that a ferry is leaving Baku (Azerbaijan) that afternoon and we can expect to be aboard on Friday evening for the return leg if all goes to plan. Obviously things do not go to plan. The 'awful' weather (beautiful blue skies with a light wind) apparently prevents the ship from leaving its harbour and we are told to sit tight and wait for a call.

Aktau is really not one of those places where one wants to 'sit tight'. Aktau and its surrounding region is oil-rich and as a result it has attracted a lot of foreign attention and investment. Russian, European and even US energy

companies have operations in this small corner of Kazakhstan and with them has come money and vast inequality.
The expats live in smart hotels and grand villas arrayed
along the shoreline (although the beach views are not
exactly Santa Monica), whilst the poorer local population
working for them live in numbered, high-rise concrete
monstrosities stacked around the rest of the town.

In our opinion, Aktau is an overpriced, charmless
place resting on its oil-rich laurels and stuffed full of
seedy-looking western oil engineers drinking away their
problems with a local Kazah girl under each arm. That
said, the 'Guns & Roses' (their favourite and seemingly
only watering hole) did become our local, and yes, we did
drink away our problems as well. Sadly our general smell
and dishevelment put off even the most adventurous of
local talent.

We fall into conversation with a pair of Scotsmen who
tell us over a game of pool and a fairly decent beer that
this is the most dangerous town in Kazakhstan. They
tell us there is a lot of resentment directed at the haves
from the have-nots and under no circumstances should
we walk the streets at night. We get the impression that
healthy outdoor pursuits are not something the average
expat working in Aktau goes in for much. Although, as
the registered owner of Netty, I get in a bit of physical
exercise one evening when I have to get the correct
stamps in our carnet de passage, which will authorise us
to make the crossing. This involves running around the
port in the pitch dark from one office to the next on
an apparently endless wild goose chase until, at last, one
officer takes pity on me and stamps it.

Now and then we check in with Ruslan, our contact
at the port – who is elusive, to say the least. He boasts

that this is because he has recently got himself a new wife – aged sixteen. This, he claims, is the explanation behind his long absences from his mobile phone. (The mind boggles.)

After three days of waiting, at 9am on a brisk Monday morning, we receive a rather abrupt phone call from him. We must report to the harbour to begin boarding immediately. The good ship *Professor Gul* is arriving in port.

We check out and hurry down to the port, ready to negotiate whatever bureaucratic maze stands in the way of getting Netty on board. In the event, it could have been worse – although we seem to require official stamps from every department from the customs office to the fire brigade.

The worst bureaucratic hurdle to overcome proves to be a twenty-dollar fine for not having the correct entry stamp for Kazakhstan. Tom has to write a handwritten letter of apology to the government for this cardinal offence – for which he deploys the most effusive and elaborate language he can dream up. This done, we are sent off with a slap on the wrist and the warning, 'If you ever do this again, there will be severe consequences, like you will never be able to come to Aktau again.' (!)

Buoyed by our relatively painless escape we head for our cabin and discover there is very little to show for the one-hundred-dollar ticket price. At least the food must be OK, we hope.

Finally, at around 10pm, we are allowed to drive Netty on board and within a couple of hours we have set sail and are heading for the open sea.

The crossing is straightforward. Contrary to our hopes, the canteen doesn't offer much besides a sort of gruel they pass off as chicken pasta. We idle away the time drinking beer and smoking with a couple of truckers – a Kazakh and an Azeri – spending hours at every meal chatting away in our respective languages with no idea what the other is saying. On the plus side, neither party ever ran out of things to say, neatly proving the point that, at the end of the day, we really just love the sound of our own voices. Picture the scene, Tom and the lorry driver each holding up an eating utensil, barking at each other in their mother tongues and laughing hysterically. 'Spoon! This is a spoon! Repeat after me! Spoon – you giant hairy infant!'

So passes many a happy hour, and by the following evening we have reached Baku. Unfortunately so had the small gusts of wind. These are enough, it seems, for the Captain to forget that he is in charge of a large cargo ship and not a small sailboat and anchors are dropped while we sit out the 'storm'. We are forced to wait for another thirty hours within swimming distance of the port.

We sit there for another whole day and a night.

Eventually, becoming bored, we wander up to the bridge. The crew are a friendly bunch although once again the language barrier is hard to overcome. Instead I try to persuade the Captain that in my country I am a renowned seaman, while Tom, on the appearance of dried pasta and chicken leg for the fourth time in a row, takes pleasure in telling the chef that he is a terrible cook. To resume our running joke, we christen everyone on the bridge, 'Phil'. Captain Phil, Radio Phil, Navigator Phil, Lorry Phil – we get to know them all, and thanks to the delay, probably a lot better than we would have liked.

Tom
We are slowly going mad. I am, anyway.

Happily, the next morning we awake at 6am to the

sound of the engines. Pretty swiftly we are docked and running Netty down the ramp into another thicket of customs procedures.

As expected, clearing them is a nightmare. Both incredibly expensive and very tedious. We manage to negotiate down our 'insurance fee' from fifty to forty dollars. But the largest expense comes through one of the most obnoxious men I have ever met. Overweight, with slicked back hair, puffy eyes and an aggressive demeanour, he wears no uniform and – to my eye – bears no outward signs of authority. Despite this, he demands an obscene amount of money from us, calculated, he says, from the length of our vehicle. Initially we simply ignore him while he shouts at us and becomes more and more irate. Eventually, after a word with 'Friendly Phil' – a Kazakh trucker – we discover the charge is legitimate. Reluctantly we traipse off to his office to do the necessary – and pay a two-hundred-and-forty-dollar charge!

'Kholodnaya, eh?' says the greasy official with a grin, clapping his shoulders to indicate that it's cold outside, which it sure is. This is his first cordial gesture, an ice breaker I assume, but it's not working.

Returning his grin, I tell him in English that it will be a lot colder when I turn the radiators off in his pokey little office. His smile broadens. I know – it doesn't reflect well on us that this is exactly what we do when his back is turned. A childish trick but it gives us both so much pleasure that we almost think the whole headache worthwhile.

Baku is an unusual place. Because of the delays being held in the harbour, we have decided not to stay even a single night here. So driving away is the only glimpse we will have of the city.

With Iran forefront in our minds we blitz it south towards the border town of Astara, passing marshland and swamps on the way. We have to be in India for Christmas and time is running out, so Azerbaijan has become the casualty.

By 3pm we are approaching the border and soon come across the inevitable queue. Hicky is driving so, unconcerned, I leave him with Netty and head off on foot to scope out the lie of the land and see what we're up against. Diplomatic relations between the UK and Iran are at a low point following the recent arrest of all Iranian nationals working in the British Embassy in Tehran so we are a little on edge.

After fifteen minutes of walking there is no sign of the border and the queue stretches unrelentingly into the distance. I come across an official and the game of pidgin charades begins. After some elaborate miming on my part met with equal enthusiasm on his, I establish to my horror that the queue is four days long. Four days! Unwittingly we have arrived during Haj – the annual Muslim pilgrimage to Mecca – and this is one of the major routes that Muslims from southern Russia, Dagestan and Azerbaijan take south. We don't have four days to spare. Every day wasted is a day less in Iran, somewhere both of us have been looking forward to since the idea of the trip was first mooted. Very disheartened, I trudge back to the car to give Hicky the bad news.

Darkness is not far off so our options are to turn back in search of a hotel or grit our teeth and get stuck in now. Bearing in mind that we haven't had a shower in three days courtesy of the sea crossing I think it is to our credit that we decide to go for the latter. We have just settled on this when an elderly Azeri man sidles quietly up to the side of the car.

'Hold up. Dodgy Phil heading our way,' says Hicky. 'I've got this.' Sure enough the man is a fixer and they get down to business.

'He says he can get us into Iran in time for tea,' reports Hicky after several minutes with the picture book.

'How much?'

'Only four hundred bucks.'

'Do we believe him?'

Hicky shrugs. 'What choice do we have?'

I agree. Hicky turns to Dodgy Phil to accept his offer but just in the nick of time I barge him aside and, in the mud caked on the side of Netty, I draw $30 with my finger and look at him with raised eyebrows. Throwing his hands to the sky, Dodgy Phil responds and with an elaborate 'Pfff!' He adds a zero to the end of $30. 'Phah!' I cry, and strike a line through his $300 and write $50. We eventually shake hands at a hundred and fifty bucks, with Hicky and I still highly sceptical that even a single dollar would be money well spent for his services. Nevertheless, we are curious to find out whether he can prove us wrong.

He points to a battered old Lada and indicates that we should follow. Pulling out of the queue we set off behind him down the side of the road. A hundred and fifty metres later our rear-view mirror fills with blue flashing lights, the wail of a siren drowns out our music and a police car pulls us both over.

No picture book is required for the ensuing bollocking. Three minutes of furious Azerbaijani diatribe follows, at which point we are sent in no uncertain terms to the back of the queue. Eyes wide, giggling nervously and wiping police spittle from our chins, we turn around, leaving

Dodgy Phil in handcuffs and considerably more trouble than us.

Resigned to our fate, Hicky heads to a garage to buy four days' worth of Azerbaijan's answer to Monster Munch, and some apples. Our goose is cooked. (Slow roasted, indeed.) Or so we thought.

Two hours later there was a gentle tap on the window, and lo and behold, Dodgy Phil is back.

I lean out of the window. 'Polizia?'

'Polizia nyet! Problema nyet!' he cries. We look at each other. We are still the last car in the queue. It's nearly dark by now. There is a long pause.

'Fuck it!' I say. 'We've nothing to lose and if we get caught we just blame Phil.' A heartbeat later Hicky agrees and we give Dodgy Phil the nod. He tells us to await full darkness. With night shortly upon us, he gives us the signal and we set off. Sure enough, there is no sign of the police and we plunge quickly into a rabbit warren of back streets and alleys, twisting our labyrinthine way through shabby districts with no street lighting. After twenty minutes we realise we are hopelessly lost and have absolutely no idea how to get back to the border. Eventually we round a corner and enter a cul-de-sac at the end of which is an unmarked green double gate and, standing either side of it, two men dressed head to toe in black and holding machine guns. The silence in our Land Rover cab is deafening.

The Lada ahead of us douses its lights and pulls over. Hicky is driving and instinctively pulls over on the opposite side of the road. A good call in my opinion. Dodgy Phil jumps out of his Lada and scurries across the road. Leaning in the window he demands his hundred and fifty.

'Not a lot of choice, as I see it,' I say to Hicky.

'Agreed. Kind of beyond committed, aren't we?'

I have the cash prepared in my pocket. I pull it out and hand it over. In the blink of an eye both the cash and Dodgy Phil are gone.

Forty-five very long and very silent minutes follow. Eventually Hicky murmurs, 'What do you think he's doing?'

'He's probably in the pub.'

Neither of us laugh.

Suddenly the gate swings open and the two guards stand to attention as a convoy of two big black Mercedes rolls past. No sooner than they're out of sight, Dodgy Phil reappears in the gateway, frantically waving us through. We slow as we pass him expecting further instruction but he just yells, 'Go! Go!' The guards turn away – literally turning their heads to look in the other direction – while we pass through the gates and find ourselves in the heart of the frontier.

Hicky

I imagine passing through Saint Peter's pearly gates must feel something like our progress through that green gate. Except hopefully the feeling lasts a bit longer. Thirty seconds later we are in the centre of the compound and looking to re-join the *main* queue which Dodgy Phil has indeed helped us to bypass. (Stupidly, I have been imagining that we will be through the entire border and into Iran in time for a non-alcoholic beverage before bed but we see now there is no way this is going to happen.) The adrenaline stays high thanks to the presence of the armed guards with AK47s stalking about the place; it turns out it needs to.

It takes another two hours of hustling to get any of the irritable Hajj pilgrims to let us back in. They huddle up bumper to bumper refusing to give us even an inch of an opening until, losing his patience, Tom jumps out of the car and plants himself in front of a pilgrim's bumper, yelling at him to give way. There is a nasty stand-off with the pilgrim's 1980s Mercedes engine gunning, shunting Tom backwards, but a gap of about two feet opens up, into which I wedge Netty's nose. In fact, I hit the gas with a little too much enthusiasm and manage to hook Netty's bull bar under the rear bumper of the lorry in front. When the lorry moves on again, Netty's nose is pulled down into the dirt and for a second it feels like the whole machine is going to be ripped in two. Suddenly, with an almighty bang, the bonnet snaps free and … breaks clear. I keep the car inching forwards as Tom jumps in the passenger side and finally we are back in the queue. We turn to look at one another, both with eyebrows raised and damp foreheads. That was intense.

The lorry driver doesn't even notice. The drivers behind certainly do – and will now have many hours to nurse their resentment.

We are now onto the next test in the border equivalent of the game show *Takeshi's Castle*. The official Azeri exit border is a large corrugated iron shack, resounding with the voices of braying pilgrims getting their passports stamped. Inside we are made to sit and wait. By now, we understand that patience is all. (Well, up to a point.) And after cutting our ordeal by several days, to wait a mere two hours while the Azeri border officials do whatever it is they want to do is no great labour. Particularly as an Azeri youth appears from nowhere and shows us exactly what we need to do.

After leaving Azerbaijan, we now have to endure five hours through a long, long night of inching our way through no man's land towards the Iranian border. I am falling in and out of sleep at the wheel, edging Netty another five inches closer to Tehran. Tom loathes this experience and will later describe it as the lowest point of the entire journey. Strangely, I don't mind it. I must still be buzzing with adrenaline and excitement that we would soon – well, relatively soon – be through and away.

When it is at last our turn to go into the Iranian customs building, my first thought is, 'This is more like it!'

For some reason, we are treated like royalty. We are ushered through with a lot of smiles and animated gesticulation in double-quick time. The Iranian border officials claim that they haven't seen a westerner since January 2008 – which I find hard to believe. In any case, we are instantly given an English-speaking border fixer – charming man – who takes us through the myriad of checks and paperwork, which includes, because we are British citizens, the taking of fingerprints. A guard arrives with a bowl of black ink into which we dunk our hands. I am oddly exuberant and full of energy. After squashing my fingers on the requisite form, I chase the hysterical guards around the facility with my inky jazz hands – as sure a sign as any that the long night has finally addled my brain.

Our unexpectedly helpful guide refuses to name a price for the assistance he has given us when it's time to tip him. We settle on twenty US dollars in a bit of a rush. Tom instantly feels guilty that it wasn't enough. 'Too late,' I shrug. The guide has already disappeared – looking for his next pair of lost souls perhaps.

By 10am the last border guard gives us a brisk salute and we pass through into Iranian territory.

We have made it.

Elation. Exhaustion.

Pilgrimtastic.

FIVE

Iran – the Noble Land

Tom

Iran? What should one expect? If our friends in the western press are to be believed, then a public lynching, ordered by an insane, bearded cleric and executed by a baying mob. In reality we find a nation of the most charming, hospitable and friendly people either of us have ever encountered. The sort of people who are interested in you for all the right reasons and for whom nothing is an inconvenience. By the end of our first day, all our preconceptions and fears have been thrown from the Netster's windows as we come to terms with our new nation of friends.

According to our guidebook, there is a concept in the Iranian national psyche which any traveller through that land must understand: *ta'arof*. This is a system of formalised politeness, which means Iranians come across, and in fact are, some of the most hospitable and welcoming people on earth.

But it can also be a little bit confusing. And our first experience of it certainly takes us by surprise.

Our border crossing fixer has told us that in Iran,

technically, we will need a special fuel ration card in order to buy petrol. (This is to prevent bootlegging of the heavily state-subsidised Iranian fuel across the border. After all, sanctions are firmly in place, so given that they can't sell the stuff abroad, they give it away cheaper than water.) However, he said we should be able to borrow a card from the attendant any time we need to fill up. Given the card is two hundred US dollars, we decide to risk it.

About twenty minutes into the country, we put this to the test. He wasn't quite right. The attendants refuse us but, at their suggestion, we manage to find a lorry driver who will let us buy fuel on his ration card. Once Netty is brim-full, the driver, who has insisted on filling the car himself, then offers to pay for it all as well. Not really grasping that this offer may have been made in the spirit of *ta'arof*, we nevertheless refuse it so many times that we do end up paying ourselves, out of sheer English awkwardness. (Perhaps as effective as *ta'arof* in ensuring that the correct people end up paying.) Still, it is hardly burdensome. We acquire over a hundred litres of fuel at the cost of a measly one dollar and fifty cents. It is worth noting that diesel has been the largest part of our daily spend so far with a hundred litres in Europe costing around $140. Not so Iran! Our hundred and twenty litres is so cheap that cups of tea are almost twice as expensive as an entire fill-up, and therefore tea replaces diesel as our most expensive fuel for the duration of our stay in Iran.

Our destination for the day is the village of Masuleh. We have read that: *'Masuleh is one of Iran's most beautiful villages.'* Which is as good a reason as any to head there for a night.

The route we take is unconventional, thanks to Hicky's unyielding aversion to ever driving the same road twice. Thus he insists we arrive from one direction in order to depart down the main road in the other. It's a drive of just over a hundred miles, initially along the Caspian coast before breaking south-west into the Talesh mountains as we adopt a circuitous route along a tiny road (on the map) which carries us up and up and up into the mountains, reducing our speed below 25mph, first through endless pine trees, then at last emerging to an expansive vista looking back north to the Caspian Sea, now thousands of feet below. The scenery is stunningly beautiful, clouds rolling over the tops of the hills, backlit by the burning sun and incredibly inviting.

We drive still higher and the conditions deteriorate into a blizzard with visibility reduced to just a few metres, the road covered in snow and Netty making good use of her chunky off-road tyres. We eventually discover this road has to crest a high-altitude pass before it then descends into Masuleh from 'on high'. As we begin our descent and drop below the snow line the road immediately deteriorates into a dirt track. We leave the snow behind. The road winds through barren brown mountains, the odd snow-capped peak in the distance the only thing breaking the monotony. There are no road signs and barely any signs of life full stop. We haven't passed another car for some considerable time now.

Our confidence waning fast, we stop to ask two shepherds the way but the language barrier proves too high, so we press on. Tucked away in the north-eastern corner of Iran, driving along a single-lane dirt road as it winds through the mountains feels indescribably remote and far from home. After several hours we spot a tiny village nestled against the hillside. We take the track that leads to the village hoping for some directions and confirmation that we are heading in the right direction. The little settlement is made entirely from mud. Within seconds of our arrival, what feels like the entire community crowd around Netty to hear why these strange foreigners have come to disturb their quiet corner of Iran.

There is much jostling, grinning, prodding and touching but eventually we get enough confirmatory nods to our repeated cries of, 'Masuleh? Masuleh?' with accompanied pointing. Happy that we are still on the right track, we press on, albeit wearily. What we thought would be a drive of perhaps an hour has already taken more than five. It is getting dark. Hicky is complaining that, after nearly five days since his last bowel movement, the time is most definitely nigh. Sure that we *must* be close to our destination, I urge him to play the man and hold on until our arrival. By now we have been up for more than two days without any sleep. Hicky is starting to hallucinate. I am utterly shattered.

Hicky
It's dark by the time we pull into Masuleh. Never have I been so quick to agree with Tom's choice of hotel and I bolt for the latrine, painfully recalling that the last time I had been was in Kazakhstan.

This is not like any other town we've been to. For a start, there are literally no roads – at least, not in the main village. Instead, the houses are built up the hillside and packed so tightly and steeply that the roof of one house provides the pathway for the next up the slope. The result is a beautiful maze of confusion.

It's evening, but there are plenty of people about.

We amble through the tiny bazaar where pretty much everyone wants to talk to us. We are slightly taken aback by their friendly nature, although we are beginning to realise that we can take this at face value. The interest is genuine. There seems to be no ulterior motive.

They all want to know where we are from and usually ask what we think of Iran. It is too soon to give an informed answer to that but we are already picking up on the huge divergence between Iran's reputation in the wider international media – as flag-burning haters and regional trouble-makers – and the experience of other travellers who have actually been there: that Iranians are the friendliest people on the planet. Perhaps that is why, wherever we go, folks are constantly wanting to be reassured that we like their country.

Based on the few hours we've been here, we do.

Petrol stations aside, this is our first proper initiation into Iranian hospitality. We stop for our first tea and a *shishah* pipe in a tiny teashop with a terrace overlooking the rest of the village, attended by a young man who clearly has Down's Syndrome. Soon after us, a larger local family arrives and scatters themselves across a few tables. They quickly persuade the waiter to perform a dance for them and he jigs around the terrace with a radio perched on one shoulder. Everyone laughs a lot.

'That's a bit low, isn't it?' I say to Tom behind my teacup.

'Not sure they care,' he replies. 'Anyway, he seems to be enjoying himself.' And it's true. The waiter is laughing louder than anyone as he goes about his rather gawky routine.

One of the daughters of the family – who speaks very good English – engages us in conversation, filtering one by one the barrage of questions being fired at us from nearly every other family member sat around the terrace. We don't last long though. After the purgatory of our night border crossing, we are too eager for the real beds that await us in our hotel.

Tom

From Masuleh we head east, tumbling out of the mountains to the valley floor and then climbing up again towards the mountaintop village of Gazor Khan, up the so-called Valley of the Assassins – made famous by Dame Freya Stark's eponymous travel diary – into thick cloud and increasingly foul weather until Netty is reduced to crawling through a blizzard, snow and slush lying thick on the road.

'It's like the opening of *Batman Begins*,' observes Hicky. (He does love a film reference.) It's certainly not going to be a drive that's easily forgotten. I find myself rather enjoying the unpredictability of the whole thing.

Gazor Khan should be a pleasant little mountain village and home to the region of Gilan's greatest attraction: Alamut Castle, of which more in a moment. But on arrival we can't see a lot. Snow is falling. We do manage to find the one and only (minuscule) guest house belonging to the friendly Ali where we are shown to an upper room in which there are three old cots in a row. One of them, we discover, is already occupied by a rather laconic Australian named Chris from Melbourne.

'Bloody hell. You get everywhere you Aussies, don't you?' Hicky observes. Chris doesn't deny it. It is certainly no mean feat of personal logistics to have found his way up to this remote spot.

Since the snow doesn't look like stopping, we decide

to tackle the staircase up the mountain to Alamut Castle at dawn the next day. We spend the evening drinking tea, guzzling huge quantities of carrot jam (a new-found personal favourite) and chatting to Chris.

In the morning, however, we discover the village is still engulfed in cloud and the snow still falling. Undaunted, we hope for the best, set our feet to the ancient staircase and begin to climb. Hicky's troublesome knee means that I end up breaking trail through the foot and a half of fresh snow.

Alamut Castle is a relic of an obscure fragment of Iranian history. From 1090 AD to 1256 AD, the fortress was held by the Shi'a Nizari Ismai'lis – one of the main sects of Islam – and was originally seized by Hasan-e Sabbah, leader of the Nizari Ismai'lites and founder of the Order of the Assassins. This was only one of several mountaintop forts that the Assassins held throughout Persia and parts of Syria, thereby creating a thorn in the side – not to mention a strategic threat – for the Sunni Seljuks who were rulers of Persia at the time. But try as they might, the Seljuk establishment could not oust their Assassin enemies from their airy strongholds. Indeed it was the Assassins who enjoyed more success – using subterfuge and covert tactics to bump off many key figures in their enemies' ranks – including a couple of caliphs, various viziers and sultans, and a few Crusader leaders for good measure. (Hence how their name has come to be used in the English language.) They seemed untouchable, and this remained the case until the Mongols invaded in the 13th century and the strongholds all surrendered. Once they had wheedled them out of their lofty aeries, the Mongols made short work of them, putting the entire Order of Assassins to the sword. Alamut Castle was left in ruins.

So much for history.

It takes us about an hour to climb to the castle. Despite the thick cloud that wreaths the landscape all around us, as we near the top it seems to me that the weather might be clearing. Sure enough, by the time we reach the castle, the cloud has completely gone. We are treated to beautifully vivid views of the castle and from there, laid out below, the entire valley and its surrounding peaks. It was undeniably glorious. The mountaintops are jagged as knives and covered in fresh snow, cutting sharply into the staggeringly clear sky above.

It doesn't last, of course. Twenty minutes later a fresh bank of cloud starts rolling in and soon everything is covered in an impenetrable fog. We consider ourselves lucky to have got even that much of a glimpse.

Hicky

The drive down from Gazor Khan is fun. The road drops like a stone from snow-covered mountain passes into dusty desert valleys in under an hour.

We have agreed to give Chris, our Aussie roommate, a lift to Tehran, which is only about sixty miles away. We drop him off around lunchtime, then push on around the Tehran ring-road.

We have long heard that driving in and around Tehran will be a baptism of fire. After an hour of several near-death experiences, a barrage of honking and untold numbers of missed turns we have the freeway in our sights and are finally on the road heading south towards Kashan.

It is a long day at the wheel – another two hundred and fifty miles further south, over three hundred and fifty in total for the day, when we roll into the city of Kashan after dark, having driven back over the same range of mountains as yesterday. Tom is lounging beside me in the passenger seat as we pull in, flicking through the guidebook.

'Listen to this,' he says. 'Apparently this city fell to the Arabs in the 7th century thanks to a bunch of scorpions.'

'What are you talking about?'

'It says here,' he reads from the book, '"Another legend tells of Abu Musa al-Ashari's novel method of taking the city of Kashan during the Arab invasion of the 7th century AD. When the Arab general found the city's walls impregnable, he ordered his men to gather thousands of scorpions from the surrounding desert. Armed with these stingers, he attacked the city by having them thrown over the walls. According to the tale the poor Kashanis, who could never have expected an attack of such diabolical genius, soon capitulated."'

'Why not just stamp on them?'

'Well, they'd sting you, clearly.'

'Drop a brick on them then.'

Tom examines the page a little further but finds nothing to answer this. 'Hmm. I dare say you can put your method to the test if you see one.'

'Can't we stay somewhere where we don't encounter anything with a fatal sting.'

'Five stars?'

'At least.'

We settle for the Golestan Inn which is at least clean. Our room looks down onto the bazaar, supposedly the biggest draw about Kashan. We go and spend some time shuffling up and down the stalls, but it's not long before we retreat to our beds. The next day we do more sight-seeing, visiting the Agha Bozorg Mosque – the first of many we are to visit in Iran – and the Khan-e Ameriha, the home of an Iranian nobleman. Built in the 19ᵗʰ century, it fell into rack and ruin and has recently been restored to its former glory. It consists of seven courtyards and covers a staggering nine thousand square metres of floor space. In its day, this was the largest home in Persia.

We are back on the road before noon and speed south towards Esfahan, arriving in this magnificent city in time for afternoon tea. According to our guidebook, one of the finest cities in the Islamic world and that is surely no exaggeration. Once we are settled into our hotel, we head for the heart of the city, Naqsh-e Jahan Square, our path taking us over a stunningly beautiful construction called the Khaju Bridge – built with double-tiered arches, part weir, part pedestrian walkway – to get us there.

Halfway across we meet a group of young people. They are wearing expensive clothes, the women all in inches of make-up. They want to chat, and more than anything want to impress us with their western credentials.

'We love Hollywood,' one declares.

'Yes. Ahmadinejad, bad. Amerika, good,' adds another.

We are starting to get a sense of the contrast in attitudes between town and country. In the towns, this kind of view seems fairly typical; the young people in particular seem more liberalised. In the country, folk are more disposed towards President Ahmadinejad, and there are photos of the various Ayatollahs all over the place.

After a stroll around its vast perimeter, we find ourselves a suitable perch in a carpet-shop-cum-tea-house over-looking the great square – also known as Meidan Emam or Imam Square. There we enjoy a bit of idle banter, taking in the sheer majesty of our surroundings. (The square is a whopping 160m wide by 560m long, most of which is filled with immaculate lawns, carefully manicured shrubs and beautiful avenues of trees.) By now, possibly with the absence of any alcohol to hand, we are both developing a serious case of sweet tooth since everywhere we go we are offered an assortment of sweet pastries, especially Zoolbia Bamieh (a kind of Persian dumpling in syrup) and Sohan Asali (another pastry made of honey, sugar, saffron and almonds). It's fair to say these become our staple for the duration of our trip through Iran.

The Imam Square draws together several characteristic aspects of Iranian culture and history. Situated on the south side of the square is the Shah Mosque (known as the Imam Mosque since the revolution). Along the western side lies the Ali Qapu Palace – the power base of the Safavid Shahs when Esfahan was the Persian capital. And at the northern end is the Keisaria gate, the entrance to the Grand Bazaar. The overall effect is rather splendid and certainly leaves the impression that this was once the centre of an immense and sophisticated civilisation.

Tom

Traces of Iran's history are found everywhere in this city. Not least in the continued existence of a thriving Armenian Quarter, reminding us that the region remains what it has always been: a melting-pot of different creeds and cultures. We read about a particular restaurant that is worth visiting in this quarter and set out in search of it, mouths watering and bellies rumbling for some traditional Armenian cuisine. After much debate and fruitless searching, we believe we have found it. We settle in for what we hope will be a memorable meal, only to be presented with a menu that includes photographs of each dish – never a good sign – none of which seems especially

Armenian, nor indeed enticing. We point at a couple of kebabs with a side order of fries. Hardly exotic fare. By the time we have finished and paid the over-priced bill, we are more than a little annoyed at the guidebook's dubious recommendation.

Only when we leave do we realise our mistake. The Armenian restaurant we were looking for is, in fact, tucked away down a staircase in the cellar beneath the place where we have just dined. We pop our heads inside. It looks wonderful.

'Balls,' is Hicky's succinct appraisal of the situation.

The next day we delve a little deeper into the cultural offerings of Esfahan, coming away with lasting impressions of the interior of the Imam Mosque – which, according to my journal, is '*absolutely* fantastic. No photographs capture the colours, the scale or the overall effect, especially when it is sitting under the most perfectly blue sky, as it was today.'

We split up to explore the Grand Bazaar. I elect to do a little more Christmas stocking shopping. By the time I leave I'm quite pleased with my haul: two plastic toy guns; one fake tattoo; one coconut; one police cap; one Iranian military dress coat; two packets of Iranian cigarettes; one set of beach paddle bats and ball.

When we meet up again, Hicky tells me he was rather taken with the bird market.

'Did you buy one?' I wouldn't put it past him.

'I was going to. But then all I could think about was cleaning bird shit off Netty's dashboard, so I passed.'

Back at the hotel, we are delighted to discover that our logistical headaches may be over – at least for a while. A family friend whose business regularly ships products around the world on cargo vessels has come to our aid.

He's offered to make the necessary arrangements for transporting Netty from the port of Bandar Abbas to Mumbai, and for a fraction of the cost that we have so far managed to negotiate for ourselves.

So, we leave Esfahan in high spirits the next morning, although there remain a few details to iron out before we have absolute certainty that we are in the clear. But hoping for the best, we change our plans, heading for the city of Yazd rather than Shiraz – on the assumption that we have gained ourselves a few extra days in Iran.

The drive carries us in a south-easterly direction across miles and miles of desert. Way out in the wilderness we pass a series of huge gun emplacements, equipped – at least to the layman's eye – with massive anti-aircraft guns. We wonder what on earth they could be defending, out in the middle of nowhere and far from any border.

'It's bound to be a nuclear site,' says Hicky. Hickman is rather a suspicious sort. He'd make a good UN inspector. But we never did find out whether he was right.

Yazd is an unusual city, unlike any other we have yet visited in Iran. All the buildings are made of mud – at least by appearance – and pedestrians get around the city by walking on the roofs of the houses, I suppose reminiscent of Masuleh.

The word *Yazd* means God – and the city was an important centre of the Zoroastrian religion throughout the span of the various Persian empires of antiquity. Even after the Islamic conquests, it continued to be so, by dint of its willingness to pay a hefty levy to its new Muslim overlords. Even today, there is still a sizeable Zoroastrian community in the city.

We pass a relaxed evening and morning in our hotel – a traditional house converted for backpackers with a friendly vibe – where we meet a Dutch couple who are to become a strangely recurring feature of the next few weeks of our journey. They tell us about a commune they have just visited some distance out in the desert. It sounds interesting. Well, to be more exact, it sounds like something between a hippy commune and an experience of the Arabian nights, which is at least interesting to us. We decide to adjust our plans accordingly.

However, before we leave Yazd we visit a few of its sites, the most memorable of which is probably the irrigation museum, which describes in great detail the qanat system. This was developed as long as three thousand years ago, whereby subterranean aquifers in the uplands of the surrounding desert valleys are redirected into underground channels, dug out of the earth and aerated by a series of access shafts, and the water is eventually brought to the surface in order to irrigate areas of land under cultivation further down the valley. (By channelling water underground it prevents evaporation before it reaches the fertile soil.)

Two things really stood out. The first was the remarkable distance these ancient engineers could make the water travel over seemingly flat ground, dropping only fractions of degrees (often 0.1% or less) in order to keep the water flowing. There are some instances of seventy-mile-long qanats, making them truly impressive feats of engineering. The other was finding out that the labourers who worked underground, digging out the hundreds of miles of tunnels to house the water channels, always wore white, for this reason: should the tunnels collapse – which they frequently did – and a labourer was buried alive, then he was at least already wearing white cloth, white being the traditional colour of an Islamic burial shroud.

Hicky

The place we are headed, Garmeh, is a date palm oasis. We have heard that the owner of the property is a mysterious man called Mazia, who furnishes his guests with homegrown hashish, rather in the manner that all other Iranian hosts furnish guests with tea. Having not had any alcohol for several days now, the promise of some sort of vice only heightens Garmeh's appeal. It's actually a fair distance north of Yazd – about a hundred and seventy-five miles through the desert.

When we arrive, we are met by Mazia's father who tells us there's no room in their guest house so we will have to camp. We are quite happy to do this, it being a while since we used the tent. We pitch camp beside a delightful natural spring at the foot of a mountain whose peak watches over the vast plateau. Beyond the green idyll of the oasis, which measures about ten acres in size, in every direction it is desert as far as the eye can see.

First things first, we put on a brew. Then, clutching our cups of tea, we scale the slope behind our campsite. At the summit, we sit and sip our tea in silence, watching the sun sink down behind the distant hills. Afterwards Tom goes off for a recce of the village, leaving me quite happy where I am.

We reconvene a little later for dinner in the guest house. All the beds have been taken by a busload of young Tehranis, for whom Garmeh is something of a liberal escape. Even by Iranian standards, this lot are particularly friendly and interested in us, so we are happy to chat until it is time to retire to our tent. All the women have removed their hijabs, which are obligatory everywhere else in the country. A sign that this is a place where they can come literally to let their hair down.

This is the first time on the trip where I see true beauty in a girl; she is stunning, but sadly my journal records only her email address and not her name, but that's beside the point, she is dark with olive skin and piercing, almost savage, eyes. A soft voice speaks fondly of her love of the UK, despite only seeing it through local propagandist TV. Well educated, she outlines the structural problems within her country and her desire to live in the west. It dawns on me that maybe in our lifetimes we might see a truly democratic Persia.

The next day, Tom has got it into his head that he wants to climb the mountain behind our campsite again before breakfast. I'm happy to leave him to it. It turns out the Tehrani tourists are leaving today, which means we will have the place pretty much to ourselves. After a lazy morning (for me, at least) we stroll out from the village, looping our track into the desert for a while. We haven't gone far when we are accosted by a band of children. Three small boys, to be precise. This proves to be one of the stranger encounters on our journey.

It starts out innocently enough. After an initial greeting I walk on while Tom is happy for them to rifle through his possessions, trying on his sunglasses, playing with his camera, listening to his iPod. I decide I'm being a bit churlish so I return to join the chat. But at this point the mood changes. These kids – bearing in mind the oldest is no more than eleven years old – start demanding money, and then, for no discernible reason, strip naked and pretend to masturbate. I confess that this is not the type of behaviour one usually sees in Norwich. I am quite shocked and find myself hoping they are taking the piss out of us rather than offering their services. Whichever, we hot-foot it out of there, wondering rather darkly whether their behaviour is linked to what previous foreigners have got up to in Garmeh. Much to Tom's amusement, the kids insist on chasing after me for some distance while he watches on, laughing his head off and taking photos of my headlong flight for the expedition record.

That afternoon we split up again. Perhaps after the somewhat salacious encounter with the locals, I feel the need for some seclusion. I retreat to a high place, back up what is rapidly feeling like 'our' mountain, armed with a paintbrush, my journal and some watercolours – there to capture the epic landscape that lay before me. True, I am at best a Sunday League water-colourist, but even I can conjure up something that resembles the great brown expanse of desert below.

Tom

Meanwhile, I drive about fifty miles out of Garmeh to visit some sand dunes in company with an Aussie (yes, another one) called Stuart. The dunes are impressive, up to a point. We scale the tallest of them – still only a couple of dozen metres high – and sit up there chatting until it begins to get dark, feeling about as far away from England as it is possible to feel.

By the time we return to the guest house at Garmeh, Mazia has bussed in another load of young Iranians. Also newly arrived are a French couple who, we discover, have been living in Tehran for the last four and a half years.

Their English is excellent. It is a welcome change to spend an evening in charming, adult conversation with them – not something we have experienced in months – sharing stories about our lives back home and the travels that have brought us to this place, while we listen to Mazia's hypnotic folk rhythms and songs. Hicky meanwhile is doing his best to chat up another doe-eyed young woman from Tehran. He doesn't get very far with her though. Probably all he deserves; when I ask him her name at the end of the evening, he can't remember it.

On this night, we stay in a room entirely constructed from mud. The simplicity of it is appealing. We unfold our rugs on the bare earth and are asleep within seconds.

From Garmeh, we chalk up a long day on the road to get us to a place called Meymand in Kerman province, which is less than five hours out from Bandar Abbas and the end of the road for us – or at least for Netty – in Iran. But our night in Meymand proves to be one of our strangest yet.

We arrive about half an hour before sunset – which turns out to be a beautiful time of day to view this extraordinary site. Meymand is a World Heritage Site, chiefly because of its unusual dwellings carved 'out of the living rock', as it were. It is tiny – a population of fewer than seven hundred – but it's gained its nod from UNESCO because it is what is called a primary human residence. Meaning that people have been living here for 12,000 years – as long as any site on the Iranian plateau. Nearly all of the residents still live in the dugout caves, some of which have been inhabited for nearly 3,000 years. One theory suggests that they were first dug out of the cliff face for religious worship, as part of the cult of Mithras, the sun god. Certainly the place must see a lot of sun. It is surrounded by desert.

Our intention is to stay the night in a 'cave hotel' – identified in our trusty travel guide – but annoyingly when we reach it, we find it is closed. While we are cursing our luck, a local lopes up to the window and tells us in extremely broken English that we are very welcome to come and stay at his house. We exchange a look. 'What the hell,' shrugs Hicky, and with a thumbs-up, we follow him up the hill.

It turns out he is the owner of two cave 'rooms': one of which serves for habitation; the other for storage. He installs us in his storage cave, a mishmash of fruit baskets, tools, blankets and various other odds and sods filling the space between the bare rock walls. There doesn't seem a lot of room for two human bodies.

'Problem?' he asks, as Hicky manfully thrusts aside a miscellany of clutter.

'No problem!' we both cry gaily.

The shock comes when we are invited into the main family cave. As he pulls aside the curtain to usher us inside, an overpowering smell hits us like a smack in the face. The place stinks like an abattoir and we soon see why. Plastic sheets have been spread all over the carpets and on top of these – leaving very little floor space for anything or anyone else – is a vast amount of freshly butchered meat. We later learn that this is the hacked-up carcass of some beast, slaughtered – or perhaps more appropriately, sacrificed – as part of the Hajj, the third day of which, unbeknownst to us, fell on that very day.

We are invited to sit down and are served tea, while our host's mother-in-law (so we gather) continues to chop up various parts of the animal (we suspect a bovid of some kind) in front of us. Meanwhile, we are getting along famously with Yasser's five-year-old twins. His wife – assuming he has a wife – is nowhere to be seen, possibly sequestered away in anticipation of our arrival (though where we cannot tell). Every now and then, the two boys crawl up to one of the pots, help themselves to another lump of meat and devour it with great dispatch.

After a while they begin to pray, so we retire discreetly to our storage cave. We're soon followed by the mother-in-law who brings us a simple but delicious supper of soup and flatbread. We tuck in, lounging on the heap of blankets which we have piled up to serve as a bed. But just as we are about to go to sleep, there is another knock at the door.

It is Yasser. He enters, stumbling a bit (whether drunk or drugged we never did find out), not exactly invited in, but we don't feel in any position to refuse him. He lies himself down on the blankets between us, an odd start. Soon Yasser's smiles become a little more leery, the more comfortable he gets between us. His attention is particularly drawn to the manly form of Hicky and he can hardly stop himself reaching out and pawing at his bicep every now and then. Yasser's English is extremely limited, and after a while our attempts to make ourselves understood in pidgin become wearisome. Instead, we turn the conversation in a more juvenile direction, mainly to amuse ourselves, since there is no sign of Yasser abandoning his quest to inveigle his way into Hicky's affections. Hickman, meanwhile, looks ever more uncomfortable with the unfolding turn of events and I'm afraid I can only look on in amusement.

Hicky, in a bold assertion of his masculinity, tells Yasser that he lives in Japan and is, in fact, a deadly Kung Fu master with not one, but two wives. Yasser only smiles at this and snuggles a little closer. Meanwhile, I relate in lurid terms the intricacies of the near-epic feuding between the potato and butternut squash farmers in Norfolk (conducted with spud-guns, naturally).

At long last, perhaps because relations between Hicky and himself aren't developing in quite the way he had hoped, Yasser's conversation falters. We seize on the moment and ask him to leave. He stumbles to his feet and bids us good night, looking rather bereft.

Once he's gone, Hicky jams the door shut with a wheelbarrow full of apples.

'You're paranoid. He's not coming back,' I say, with a yawn.

'I wouldn't put it past him. Dirty bugger.'

'You flatter yourself, my friend.'

Even so, the wheelbarrow stays there all night.

Hicky

We are away early next morning – after a breakfast of lamb stew and sheep's feet, what else? – on our way to Bandar Abbas, perhaps having not fully appreciated the unique experience of spending a night in those ancient cave dwellings. Still, I for one feel relieved.

It is a slow drive down there – through winding mountain roads which eventually tumble down onto the flatter, hotter coastal plain of the Persian Gulf. There is little to report about Bandar Abbas. Our two days there are taken up mainly with playing cat and mouse with our elusive shipping agent, with whom we do eventually catch up at the Hormoz Hotel, and who relieves us of the necessary paperwork to see Netty safely through customs and on board her ship. It is a strange sensation to be parted from our trusty machine, but there is an undeniable sense of euphoria to know that Netty is now on her way to India – and all for the relatively modest sum of $440. (Compare that with the $2,500 we almost got landed with.)

As for us, our plan is to hightail it to Shiraz as a final port of call before leaving Iran. The shipping agent finishes up depositing us at the bus station, having procured for us a one-way ticket to Shiraz.

'Best service ever,' comments Tom, as we wave the agent goodbye through the window.

'Absolutely,' I agree, feeling thoroughly satisfied.

Except we speak a little too soon.

The next ten hours are hell. I am not, and I suppose I never will be, much of a backpacker. This bus journey merely confirms that opinion. Offensive bus conductors, two women seated behind us producing quite astonishing quantities of vomit throughout the journey, and – having arrived in Shiraz at 4am, broken men – being told we are not allowed into the room in our hotel until 6am, all of this is sufficient to convince me never to attempt anything so ill-conceived again.

Not even the famous rose-flavoured sorbet – known as *faloodeh* – procured in the main central square, can win us over to Shiraz. It has the feel more of a western city, very modern but with far less charm than the other cities we have visited. Perhaps for that reason, it's the place that leaves the least impression. In the end, we will spend five days here, which at the time feels far too long. Both of us end up getting itchy feet and become irritable, knowing that Iran has come to an end and that a new country beckons.

Nevertheless, there are some memorable moments.

On the first afternoon, having caught up on some sleep, we sally forth into the city. On our return, we are accosted by a young Iranian man we call Iranian Phil. His English is excellent. He is a student. He offers to show us where he is studying – the Khan School – from which, he claims, there are great views of the city. Ennui, at least in my case, leads us to accept his offer.

Sure enough, he leads us up onto the roof of the school and we are treated to a great panoramic vista over the city. At this point, he offers to take us to something he calls the Holy Shrine which he has pointed out from the rooftop. He claims it is only open until 2pm on one day of the week. It just so happens that today is the day.

So he guides us around this Holy Shrine. It is undeniably impressive, the interior decorated with gorgeously elaborate and intricate green glass mosaics. Men are at prayer. (The women are elsewhere, in a separate section.) We agree it has a pretty extraordinary atmosphere. The reverence of the worshippers is almost palpable.

On the third day, we take a day trip out to the famed city of Persepolis. Tom seems to know all about it from his Ancient History degree days. 'It was the ceremonial capital of the Achaemenid Empire from the 6th to the 4th century BC,' he intones during our taxi ride out there. 'It was built by King Darius the Great—'

'Was that the cross-dresser in *300*?' I interject.

At this point, Tom abandons his history lesson.

On arrival, I concede it is a privilege walking around with someone who knows what they are talking about. We later meet some other tourists who think Persepolis is a massive let-down. Which only goes to show, there's no pleasing some people.

The site is remarkable. We wander around gawping at the columns still standing, of which there are many; the royal tombs carved into the rock-faces; the massive ruins of the various grand buildings that they constructed – military barracks, a treasury and the other ceremonial palace buildings associated with the Shah. The various bas-reliefs still remaining are equally impressive, and perhaps most magnificent of all is the Gate of All Nations

— still standing twenty-five metres tall after well over two thousand years, and flanked by two enormous *lamassu* (bulls with the heads of bearded men).

After the splendour of Persepolis, we become even more irritable once back in Shiraz. Our mood is not helped when we decide, for lack of anything better to do, to revisit the Holy Shrine again, and discover that it is possible to visit not only on any day of the week but also for free. Oh well, another forty dollars lifted unnecessarily from our ingénue pockets. I suppose the fact that this is the first time this has happened since somewhere back in Russia says something about our progress — and the rest of Iran.

That being said, both of us get a little weary of the relentless, 'Hello, where are you from?' from any passerby. This weariness is probably a sign that we are in need of a break. Or at least a drink. Still, for all that, our final evening in Shiraz is somewhat redemptive. We return to a particular tea and *shishah* house which we have visited a couple of days before. It is full of young Iranian men, so we have to share a carpet with one pair already seated and puffing away. It's not long before they engage us in conversation and offer us their *shishah* to share. Indeed, not only them, but three other pairs of smokers want us to smoke with them. It proves to be a thoroughly entertaining evening and by the time we leave, our moods are fully restored, as is our love and respect for all things Iranian.

Well, most things Iranian.

All that remains is to negotiate the airport. Easily done — albeit with an hour's flight delay, which will prove fortuitous once we hit Bahrain. As the wheels of our plane leave the ground, Tom puts out his hand. We shake, grinning like fools. It's a good moment. Nothing needs to be said.

SIX

———

India – Pandemonium and Bliss

Hicky

Before we are to be reunited with Netty and plunge into the pandemonium of the subcontinent, we have planned to spend three days in Dubai. After the penitent life of a Muslim the last three weeks, this proves the perfect place to reacquaint ourselves with the more decadent pleasures that the austere Islamic Republic shuns (at least in theory). Yes, it was alcohol that was first on our minds and lips – although thankfully there is little photographic evidence of the ensuing couple of days. Goodbye to the subtlety and splendour of Persia. Hello to … well, something very different.

The unleashing, as it were, begins on the flight over there. A delay leaving Shiraz means we have several hours to kill in transit in a Bahrain airport business lounge. There, our parched tongues receive ample refreshment, to the point that when we finally take our seats on the plane bound for Dubai we sink into blissful, beer-sodden oblivion at once.

If rest is what we need, we are certainly to get plenty of it in Dubai. Rest, and recreation.

Our sojourn in Dubai is not really part of this story, other than as a way station where we mark time while Netty forges bravely ahead to India by sea – a fact that rarely leaves my mind since I am responsible for her safe arrival. This will cause me not a little anxiety during the days before we lay eyes on her again.

However, there is plenty in Dubai to distract a man from even his worst fears. If Iran was an impressive exercise in restraint (for the most part), Dubai is no holds barred. Tom has a cousin – another one – living in Dubai who kindly puts us up for the duration of our stay. Her boyfriend is between jobs and dedicates himself with remarkable resolution to showing us a good time. Most of what this involves loses sharpness in my memory in a kind of haze of alcohol, but one event in Dubai does stick.

Somewhere around the middle of December, we attend an event at one of Dubai's many business hotels. You know the ones – several hundred stories high and with a foyer you could park a jumbo jet in. The event is billed as a 'bottomless brunch' – with a Christmas theme of course. Black tie is requisite despite the 11am kick-off. What ensues is three hours of skulling champagne out of Christmas hats and the odd plate of food (though I don't remember much of that), while waiters waft around with large scorecards declaring last year's total consumption of champagne and a running total of this year's attempt to beat it. Needless to say, there is much commitment from this year's crowd not to be outdone.

With all this bonhomie well underway, we happen to cross paths with Chris Cairns, the world-renowned (at least in some circles) New Zealand cricketer. Not one to miss an opportunity to rub shoulders with the sporting elite, I grab Tom and sidle up to Mr Cairns.

'Chris, old boy,' I say, raising my glass. 'Would you be kind enough to down a glass of champagne with us?'

'Sure, mate,' comes the laconic reply.

'Let's toast the English, eh?' (One can but try.)

Mr Cairns laughs. 'No way, mate. Here's to big tits.'

We shrug agreeably and down it goes.

Tom

We are on a late-night flight to India which, thanks to yet more delays, has us arriving in Mumbai airport around 4:40am on December 15th. Most of the organisation of this part of the trip has been left to Hicky, as he says. Anticipating that Netty will be waiting for us somewhere near the port, he has booked us a room in a hotel in the district of Navi Mumbai.

This 'new city' is some distance from the airport, but nothing could have prepared us for the protracted and painful journey to reach our bed. Well, I say that – I have been to India before. Hicky has not. My impression from that trip was this: fifty per cent loved it; fifty per cent not so sure. As anyone used to western efficiency who has been there knows, India's ways can be frustrating, if not infuriating. Hicky is introduced to this fact almost immediately.

From the airport, we jump into an antiquated 'Black Cab' – an anachronism which at first delights Hicky until about a mile after departure when one of the wheels falls off. Literally. We all get out. The driver takes a look at the empty space where his wheel used to be. 'Oh, no problem, sir. Five minutes, five minutes,' he assures us, waggling his head side to side in that beautifully characteristic gesture of the subcontinent.

Half an hour later, we are no discernibly closer to

moving. It's now 5:35am. Hickman starts swearing.

'Here it is, my friend,' I say, patting his shoulder.

'Here is what?' he responds grumpily.

'Your introduction. Welcome to India.'

Eventually we give up waiting and jump on a passing tuk-tuk scooter with all our luggage and endure a two-and-a-half-hour bump and grind through the pandemonium of who-knows-which districts of outer Mumbai to reach our hotel in Navi Mumbai. It's now just after 8am. At least we are in the right place to deal with Netty's release, or so we think. However, once we get our local import agent, Aubrey, on the phone, we are dismayed to learn that all the necessary arrangements for Netty to clear customs must be carried out in various offices in the centre of Mumbai. So much for Hicky's organisational skills.

It seems we have both badly underestimated the snare of bureaucracy from which we must disentangle our beloved Netty in order to get back on the road.

There follows a series of days in Mumbai, relocating hotels, amusing ourselves, taking in a few sites and traipsing from pillar to post at the behest of the agent, Aubrey, in order to get the necessary sign-offs (and effect the necessary pay-offs) which will eventually release our trusty Netster back into our possession. Aubrey, our 'fixer', is a rather splendid character – gloriously fat, constantly sweating, palming back an unruly shock of dyed-orange hair, and unfailingly dressed in shirt and tie. The tie is always loose; the shirt is always half-soaked through with sweat, no matter what time of day. He is the soul of dishevelment. The consummate import agent. And completely charming. As to his efficiency, we can only judge him on the fact that Netty will eventually be returned to us in one piece.

While all this *baksheesh* (greasing of palms) is set in motion, we spend a few days kicking our heels in downtown Mumbai. One afternoon, walking back to our hotel after a very satisfying lunch in a canteen owned by probably the most enthusiastic monarchist in all of India, we are stopped on the street by a film scout. He is looking for western extras for the next big Bollywood blockbuster and we fit the bill. Would we be available for filming tomorrow?

'Do we get paid?' asks Hicky.

'Of course, sir,' the scout nods with alacrity. He proudly presents his business card on which is blazoned: 'Imran Giles – of *Casting Planet Agency for Foreign Models*' – in support of his credentials.

We look at each other and shrug. 'Sure, let's do it.'

'Excellent.' He hands Hicky a scrap of paper. 'We pick you up at seven thirty tomorrow morning from that address.'

Hickman grins. 'Bollywood, here we come.'

Hicky

We are there at 07:30 sharp the next day, along with twenty other westerners with equally empty agendas for that day. A minibus pulls up; we all pile in, utterly trusting that it is taking us to the shooting location. (I remark to Tom that it could be driving us off to a concentration camp for all we really know.)

Happily, it doesn't.

On arrival, we find ourselves on a shooting lot, surrounded by large warehouses. We are assembled and introduced to the assistant director who will be telling us what to do throughout the day. Almost immediately, she asks whether any of us have any experience ironing. As in clothes. A random question, to be sure, but two hands shoot up so fast that all others are deterred. No one gets a look in.

The irony of this is that our combined experience is... well, all Tom. And even that was only a measly few weeks ironing business shirts during his lonely job placement living in a Best Western in Cardiff. Winging it as always, before we know it, Tom and I have been elevated from the ranks of lowly background extras to the dizzy heights of being in shot as foreground extras, flanking the Bollywood mega-star Shahid Kapoor in the unforgettably named *Badmaash Company*. (Taran Adarsh of 'Bollywood Hungama' gave it a solid rating of 3 out of 5 stars.) We are 'part of a montage,' we are told. In a couple of sentences: the film is a love story. The male lead is chasing his lost lady-love to New York City and finds himself out of pocket and working in a New York 'sweatshop' owned by a corrupt Indian businessman. This requires ironing. Which is where we come in.

Before the actual ironing shot commences, the camera director, apparently spotting a talent amongst the throngs of extras, asks me to shout for a coffee in my best Irish-American accent as part of the scene. I wonder whether I have found my calling? Meanwhile, she wants to frame the shot with us in it, so she positions us with our irons and ironing boards either side of an empty place.

(The star will join later. In true diva style, he is half an hour late, demands his special 'drink', swigs it back, and promptly spits it out again in disgust all over his assistant.)

The AD tells us to start ironing and yells, 'Action!'

Tom

Almost immediately she shouts, 'Cut.' At first, I'm not sure why but I see from the direction of her gaze and the look on her face that the problem lies with us. I glance over at Hicky and the reason becomes clearer. It's no great claim I know, but I have over the years – mainly in hotel rooms with work the next day – learned how to iron a shirt. Hicky clearly has not. Rather than using the tried and tested method, adopted worldwide, of running the iron smoothly over a shirt that is stretched over an ironing board, Hicky has placed the whole shirt on the board and from a height of about three feet is dabbing at the crumpled shirt below.

I am stunned. Up until this moment, I had no idea that Hickman was quite so inept. I mean, don't get me wrong – I'd a pretty good inkling that ironing is not something that Hicky goes in for on a regular basis. But that he has no concept of how an iron should be used is, frankly, beyond the pale.

The AD, meanwhile, is addressing Hicky. 'Stop, stop, stop. I'm sorry, sir – but have you ever ironed anything before?'

Hicky is turning a deep shade of purple. But perhaps not in the way you might think. 'How dare you suggest such a thing?' he thunders in full indignation. 'Of course, I've ironed before! What do you take me for? This is how we do it in England.' His bravado is a thing of great wonder. 'I mean, if you want me to iron this thing some *other* way,' he adds, in a more conciliatory tone, 'that's fine. Just tell me how you would like it done and I'll do it your way.' This is a strong play from Hickman, I have to admit.

'Erm, yes sir. Please,' says an obviously chastened

AD. The look on her face, caught so totally off guard, is hilarious and I smother my giggles. 'If you wouldn't mind to do it using the more – erm – *traditional* method. Putting the shirt down flat and running the iron over it, like so...' She demonstrates.

'Of course, no problem,' replies Hicky, now the soul of compliance. 'Like I said, I'm happy to do it anyway you like.' And away he goes.

This settled, Hickman has his moment to shine and gets to deliver a couple of choice lines of dialogue: demanding a coffee in a thick Boston accent. Inevitably, when said coffee arrives he can't resist an ad lib, taking an imaginary sip before loudly declaring it disgusting. Cue another 'Cut!'

By the end of the day, we have been on set for nearly ten hours, for which we are paid the princely sum of five hundred rupees. At the time this works out at just over fifty pence an hour. But then you can't put a price on experience, I suppose.

Hicky

After our inauspicious beginnings, I do come to like Mumbai in the end. All the same, we are still elated when Aubrey tells us that Netty is finally ready to be discharged. It's December 21st, a Monday morning. We take the ferry from India Gate to Nhava Sheva at 8am. We can't help noticing that every single passenger is wearing a life jacket, and briefly wonder whether they know something about the sea-worthiness of our vessel that we don't.

It is one of those thick hazy Asian mornings. Dawn sunlight filters through the smoke and smog, shimmering off the oily waters and bathing everything in ethereal light.

A delicious feeling of anticipation rises up inside me. We'll be underway very soon.

At the port, the reunion is simple enough. However, relief to see dear old Netty soon evaporates into frustration and eventually boredom when several hours later the custom official has yet to materialise for the final inspection and to release us into the open arms of whatever life on the Indian road has to offer. We pass the time laying out our deck furniture and making up an impromptu picnic on the concrete. We snack away, watching the port traffic come and go, surrounded by dust and discarded reefers. At last he appears, and after all that, his inspection is over in a couple of minutes. We are free.

We head south at once and batter our way out of the city's traffic-clogged limits. We have been driving in India for only half a day and already we agree it's the worst traffic in the world. By the time we reach our hotel for the night, somewhere innocuous just south of Mumbai, we are cooked. Overwrought, exhausted and probably half-poisoned by traffic fumes. Technically, traffic drives on the left-hand side of the road in India, though you wouldn't know it from the last few hours we have spent on the road. But we are at least on our way.

The next day our phone rings.

'I'm very sorry to disturb, sir,' says the hotel concierge. 'But you need come quickly. Your car has terrible problem. There is some liquid leaking all over.'

'No, it does that,' says Tom, rolling his eyes. 'It's fine.'

'But it is truly very bad. You must come, I think.'

Our room is seven floors up. We go to the window and look down on Netty. We see that the small damp patch we are used to leaving behind us has in fact swelled into an expansive (and growing) lake of diesel.

'Hmm,' Tom muses. 'Perhaps we had better take a look.'

Dramatic as it looks, the problem, it turns out, is not critical: the result, most likely, of our filling Netty up to the brim the day before, after having been required to drain her completely of all fluids for her sea voyage. Even so, a crowd of locals has gathered, more than a little trepidatious of our sparking the ignition, expecting – perhaps hoping – to witness the unusual spectacle of two English eccentrics being engulfed in a raging fireball. In the event, this doesn't happen.

Instead, once we've set out, a glorious feeling of promise swells in my heart. The windows are down, my feet are propped on the wing-mirror, I have a cigarette lit and some of the usual Brit Pop is blaring out of the speakers. We feel like old hands at this now. The scenery is sometimes stunning – up and down through lush green forests threading back and forth to the seashore. We are following the coast road south – a single carriageway that runs the full length of the western side of India and will carry us down the coastline, leapfrogging an almost unbroken series of beaches – some decidedly more appealing than others. However, for now our short-term goal is to reach Goa where we plan to spend two weeks with friends who have flown out to meet us, as well as celebrate Christmas.

We are heading for a place called Ganpatipule, a beach on the guidebook's trail. However, owing to a discrepancy on our map, we discover that the road we are expecting to get us across a wide river to reach our destination for the night in reality does not exist. Instead we stay on the north side of the estuary in a smaller town called Velneshwar.

The hotel we find by the beach is very basic. But we

nevertheless enjoy a pleasant evening chatting with the owner. An educated man – and possessor of no fewer than two degrees – he talks expansively about India's history, his views on the consequences of British rule and many other subjects. But nothing seems to exercise him quite so irksomely as the rising wages of his staff. Things have got so bad, he explains, that he is now having to pay each of his staff as much as $5 a month. Outrageous! We sympathise with him most heartily.

When we retire to our £2.50-a-night room, Tom flicks on the light, only to discover a large red toad sitting on his pillow. When he tries to cajole it off his bed, the thing jumps at him and he screams so loudly that the local staff come running, thinking something awful has happened. They remove the unwanted intruder. Later, although Tom can't identify the exact species of his batrachian nemesis, he tells me he is certain that it was venomous.

'It's a law of nature,' he explains. 'Red markings on amphibians mean they are venomous.'

I remain sceptical. 'Perudo?' I say.

(Our way of calling bullshit.)

Tom

After Velneshwar, our next stop is a beach called Tarkalit, a day's drive south. Breathtaking: huge, brilliant white sand, hardly any people around and – unusually – very little rubbish. We both feel we may have peaked too early and that Goa could prove something of a disappointment after such a treat. We splash around for hours in the beautifully warm surf, diving after the now infamous Queen's Club Tennis Ball (this is allowed out for special occasions) and playing paddle in the shallows. Hicky befriends some local kids playing around the vestiges of an old fishing skiff pulled up on the beach. There follows a spot of 'cultural exchange'. They teach us some Indian dance moves; Hicky imparts one or two breakdancing moves and a perfect rendition of the Macarena.

These are glory days on the road – cruising south down the coastline with the temperature rising all the time. We reach Goa on December 24th. Christmas Eve. In the event, stood against Tarkalit it *is* a disappointment, though we can hardly complain.

We have treated ourselves to a 'luxury hotel' – the Fort Aguada Beach Resort in Goa – over the Christmas period and we arrive in good time on Christmas Eve to take full advantage of whatever luxuries the place has to offer.

We are paying extra for the first night because all the guests are invited to a Christmas Eve Gala Dinner. We skip lunch to ensure our bellies are ready for this festive all-you-can-eat extravaganza. And true to its billing, the evening is rather impressive. Dinner is served up on a hill above the main hotel in a series of marquees and terraces and palm trees all immaculately decorated with fairy lights, reindeers, Father Christmases and sundry other decorations, enough to satisfy the most demanding of Christmas die-hards.

We enter into the festive spirit with great aplomb – partaking of the copious quantities of food and drink. To excess, naturally. Before long Hicky has launched himself onto the dance floor where he terrorises many people, not least the hotel's pantomime Father Christmas, several octogenarians and a local businessman, whose daughter Hicky seems determined to dry-hump into the New Year. Whether this ended well or badly, I cannot tell you, because the next thing I remember is waking up in our room at 5am.

The stench is beyond description.

'Oh god, Hickman,' I groan. 'Were you sick?'

Hicky's prostrate figure stirs and utters something inarticulate. After more prodding he does at last speak, confessing he remembers no more than me. Desperate times call for desperate measures (or maybe it was a stroke of genius). I call room service and order a bottle of champagne, which is duly delivered and after seeing away most of that, we can at least sit upright and communicate.

Sleep is not an option – the room smells too bad – so we throw open the windows and decide the moment has arrived to open our Christmas stockings. This is great fun, and proves more nostalgic than anything else, reminding us of the places we have been so far, each item still wrapped in whatever cheap plastic bag from whichever flea market it came from. Slovakia, Hungary, Romania, Ukraine, Russia, Kazakhstan, Iran. We relive them all. Here's the list:

> a hash pipe; a Russian soldier's fur hat; a Kazakh corporal's replica tunic; Ukrainian Y-front briefs; a scarf made of rat fur; a piece of string; a thermometer; two plastic toy guns; one fake tattoo; one coconut; one police cap; one Iranian military dress coat; two packets of Iranian cigarettes; one set of beach paddle bats and ball.

By this stage it is about 7am and the sun is coming up. My eye falls on my camera beside my bed and I suggest we flick through the shots from last night's entertainment. We are most surprised to discover a whole sequence of photos taken in the room which record, in more detail than anyone would like, the final moments of Hickman's demise before we fell asleep. Not a pretty way to start Christmas Day.

Feeling somewhat unclean, we hie ourselves to a church.

By the time we rouse ourselves from our torpor and find a likely establishment – a Portuguese Catholic church, naturally enough in Goa – the service is already well underway. At first we are a little disappointed that we appear to have missed most of the Christmas Day service. Two hours later, however, the congregation is still in full voice and with no discernible sign of bringing proceedings to a close. In the meantime, Hicky has had to absent himself, not once but twice, in order to be sick outside.

Despite our woeful state, and against all the odds, we have a social engagement for Christmas lunch. My girlfriend's sister and some friends are in Goa for a wedding, and we are meeting on the beach. We meet. We eat. We survive. Before then scurrying back to our own hotel room where I take the worst decision of the trip. For supper, I order a 'chicken burger'. A serious lapse of judgement but I am desperate for some junk food to ease the pain of the hangover. Even Hickman knows not to indulge in western cuisine in India.

My chicken burger arrives in the form of a minced patty (which should have forewarned me). I wolf it down, together with all its accompanying garnishes, including the unidentified parasite which will plague me, on and off, for the next three months.

Hicky
In the end we spend just over two weeks in Goa. It is

pleasant, as all who have been there will report. Tom's girlfriend, brother and a mutual friend have flown out to be with us, and we enjoy two weeks of the hippy lifestyle that all westerners come to Goa to experience.

We put them back on the plane on January 14th and head south again. By way of experiment, when we leave Goa we try some night-time driving, never to be repeated. Indian drivers' propensity to treat the left-hand-lane rule more as a guideline than an actual requirement makes driving in the dark a truly hazardous endeavour, not made any easier by the fact that the majority of lorries don't have functioning headlamps. Often the only indication that a large vehicle was bearing down on us at lusty speed was a single LED light perched on the bonnet. At least we learn our lesson.

We bowl down the coast, stopping in at various recommended beaches. Each one starts to roll into the next. Benaulim, Gokarna, Om, Malpe. We see them all in turn – enjoying tasting baby hammerhead shark, playing endless games of paddle-ball on the beach, and the cooling sea-breeze on the road. The only flies in this otherwise pleasant ointment are the western hippies whom we encounter at each stop. I suppose there is a danger of feeling a little at odds with these characters. But the propulsive sense of purpose we have – the goal of making it all the way round the globe – seems in marked contrast to the drifting languor of the average traveller in that part of the world. Perhaps it's this feeling of difference – let's call it non-alignment – that makes us decide on a rather drastic course of action, namely shaving our heads. We feel that this is a statement that we are not them.

The transformation from gentleman traveller to England football away fan is quickly achieved. Thereafter, there can be no doubt that we are definitely *not* running with the dreadlocked pack.

The first real break from the coast comes when we head inland for Mysuru, better known – to us at least – as Mysore, one of the old provincial capitals of the Raj, and capital of the Kingdom of Mysore until as recently as 1956. The British are, of course, long gone by the time we take a look round the old decaying government building. However, there is at least one splendid colonial moustache in evidence, vestige of a bygone era, which puts Tom's measly efforts firmly in their place.

On the way we pass three days trekking in the hills around Madikeri, a hill station town. This is an unforgettably magical experience, providing us with some much-needed physical exercise under the Indian sun after the lassitude of our endless beach tour. This is trekking as it should be, with no sign of paths or tracks, other than wild animal trails we cross from time to time. Vinoe, our tirelessly enthusiastic guide, points out the wild spices and plants we pass on the way which include coffee, cardamom, vanilla, wild tobacco, papaya, betel nut (as used in paan, the ubiquitous Indian delicacy that stains bright red so many mouths and teeth in that country) and tea, to name but a few.

There's plenty to see in Mysuru as well. We find it less claustrophobic than some of the other cities we visit. Our hotel is next to a fruit-and-veg market where all the produce is wheeled in and out each morning on handcarts by wiry men who spend the rest of the day hawking their wares at the top of their voices. The abundance of sacred cows, sprayed with yellow paint, wandering the streets also never fails to bring a smile to one's face.

As far as sites of interest go, the main spectacle is the

great Mysuru Palace, which twice a week for an hour at a time is lit up with ninety-six thousand light bulbs; the sight made Harrods look very small indeed. The fact that for thirty miles around every Indian home is plunged into darkness is a not-sufficient reason to discontinue the tradition, it seems.

From Mysuru we head for the hill station of Ooty, which lies just under a hundred miles due south of the city, close to the southern tip of the Mudumalai National Park. Ooty is famous for its tea plantations and was a popular summer and weekend getaway for the British during the Raj, elevated and cool as it was – not to mention set in stunningly beautiful surroundings.

The drive up there is epic – possibly one of the most memorable of the entire trip – the road snaking its way up into the Nilgiri Hills ('Blue Hills') which pile up, ridge after ridge, on either side of the road, mist swirling in skeins off their peaks. Closer to the eye, the road is lined with immaculately manicured box hedges, all maintained by hand and which serve as perimeters to the tea plantations which have operated in this region for nearly two centuries. The landscape is serene. It is with good reason that Ooty is known as the Queen of the Hill Stations.

Ooty is situated in the Nilgiri Biosphere Reserve. As such it is replete with places of natural beauty – gardens, parks, lakes, dams and forests. Our hotel sits next to Ooty Lake itself, and in the afternoon of our arrival we venture out onto the water on a pedalo with a couple of beers and a pack of cards. Several of the other pedalos, manned by Indians, sidle up alongside us, not very subtly, and the folk on board proceed to stare at us in that uniquely Indian way – with no compunction whatsoever – simply observing the foreigners and what they are up to.

We do some more trekking in Ooty, around the tea and spice plantations, although it is considerably less taxing than the trekking we have just done in Madikeri. At one point, our guide stops us for lunch at a labourer's shop. ('Restaurant' would be far too grand a word for it.) We are treated to some of the most delicious dhal we have ever tasted, all served off a tablecloth of yesterday's newspapers – apparently a luxury only afforded to the 'garas' – foreigners. Everyone else has to make do eating off a wooden bench.

Everywhere and everything in Ooty is reminiscent of the Raj. It was, after all, founded by a pair of Englishmen soon after 1820. Although we are staying in another fleahole hostel, we decide to stroll up the street to the Savoy Hotel for dinner. When in Rome, right? (Happily, providing me with an opportunity to sport my rather natty Ukrainian corporal's jacket, although sadly I had 'misplaced' the matching Y-fronts.) Alas, Ooty's Savoy is not quite so polished as its London namesake, but it is smart, nevertheless, with oak-panelled hallways and dining rooms, covered verandas, immaculately attired waiters and rum toddies to see us off to bed. Entering into the spirit of things, I decide to take us back to the days of the Raj, we start with gin and tonics, move onto the Châteauneuf-du-Pape and we each order a Steak Diane.

'I'd forgotten just how good that can be,' says Tom, leaning back into his wicker chair and patting his sated belly. (A brave action considering the state it's been in.)

'What do you mean?'

'The pleasure you can get from a glass of good red wine and a steak.'

'Indeed. You know, I think colonial life would have rather suited me.'

He smiles. 'You sadly look more like a member of the Barmy Army, my friend.'

He's undoubtedly right.

Tom

We continue south to Munnar – another well-known hill station – which, legend has it, was first prospected by Arthur Wellesley (later Duke of Wellington) in his military manoeuvres against the Tipu Sultan towards the end of the 18th century. Sadly the dates of his known whereabouts don't bear this out, though it makes a good story. Munnar means 'three rivers', at the confluence of which this hill station is situated. I am simply blown away by the sheer beauty of the land we are driving through. Perfectly groomed tea plantations (that more closely resemble box hedging than a profitable farming crop) deck shapely hills in lush varieties of green, before the hills themselves seem to tire of their mantle and spring up into vertical cliffs, giving them a far more inspiring or impressive look than any mountains of similar height that I have seen before.

Hyperbole, perhaps. But there are two centuries of visitors to this land who would back me up. These mountains are the Western Ghats – a UNESCO World Heritage Site, and one of the eight 'hottest hot-spots' of biological diversity on the planet. As if to prove the point, we round a corner and run into a family of elephants (not literally, of course), which are feeding off the trees hardly twenty metres from the bonnet of our car. The serenity, both inside and out, causes me to reflect on how fortunate I am to be on this adventure, on how different my life is now to what it was eight months ago. Some comparisons pop into my mind as we are driving along. I jot them down in my journal later that evening:

- Uniform: Shorts & sunglasses
- Office: Cab of a Land Rover
- Boss: Myself (with due consideration for Hicky)
- Deadlines: Self-imposed and 100% flexible
- Most commonly found: With feet out of the window, listening to music & playing air guitar
- Favourite day of the week: EVERY SINGLE ONE OF THEM!

I think we can term this 'Wanderlust Euphoria'. A common enough condition, to be sure, but no less delightful for that.

In Munnar we pass a couple of days variously visiting tea plantations, walking, seeking out waterfalls, breathing in the crystal-clear air, surviving near-death experiences on hired bicycles, etc., etc.

From here, we move on to Kumily, another hill station, where Hicky's parents are waiting to spend a week with us. Needless to say, the hotel in which we all stay is a cut above the £2.50-a-night accommodation we've been used to further north. And after a week in probably the most comfortable bed I've slept in since England, when it's time to leave, I feel more relaxed than at any point on the trip so far.

We are pushing on towards the tip of India now. Back to the coast to Varkala beach, where we are amazed to run into our old companions of the road, Martin and Manon, the Dutch couple whom we have bumped into four times now, since our first meeting all the way back in Iran. When we leave Varkala for Kovalam we give them a lift. Every day is a blaze of bright blue sky now. It is hot.

The sea is the clearest we have encountered thus far, and the beaches blissfully free of development. Virgin sands, as it were – with the restaurants and beach huts where we are staying set back on the cliff tops above.

These are my thoughts until we reach Kovalam, which is the opposite of all of this. And almost immediately we decide to move on after only one night. The following day we reach Cape Comorin.

It's not every day you can say you've driven the length of India (more or less), having covered almost exactly 1,000 miles since leaving Mumbai. The novelty of being able to stand on the southernmost point of the subcontinent is somewhat marred by the two-and-a-half-hour queue we have to endure to take the ferry to the temple which marks the spot. Like the other pilgrims to the temple, we wander around bare-chested – which seems to be requisite. The other Indian day-trippers are as over-excited as ever and their enthusiasm is infectious. We mark the end of this leg of our journey through India by paying homage to the great man himself – Gandhi's memorial stands in splendour, gazing out over the Indian Ocean.

'I just realised,' says Hicky. 'This is halfway, more or less.'

'Seems like a good place to mark it.'

'So from now on,' he grins, 'we're heading home.'

'Yeah. Strange thought.'

SEVEN

India – Saints & Sinners

Hicky

We now have a couple of days of hard driving ahead to reach a town called Mamallapuram, just south of the city of Chennai. However, our first waypoint from the cape is the temple town of Madurai, lying about 230km north.

We are excited because this is the first time since the city of Mumbai that we have the boon of a dual carriageway to drive on. We set off at our usual break-neck speed of 62mph, Netty's engine purring along. Expressway N7 is completely empty. That is until Tom notices a speck on the horizon, growing larger. It continues to do so at a rapid rate until all of a sudden he has to swerve violently into the other lane, narrowly missing a horse and cart ambling along in the *opposite* direction in the fast lane of the main expressway heading north. The disregard for the fundamentals of the highway code is absolute, it seems. This conclusion is further confirmed over the next section of our journey as we encounter various other slow-moving traffic heading straight for us: tractors, lorries, diggers, livestock, more carts, bicycles – you name it. We adopt the judicious approach and return to a more sedate 40mph, hitherto our usual speed.

Nevertheless, the direct line that the N7 cuts up to Madurai still allows us to cover the 230km in something under four hours.

Although we are there for only a night, Madurai will leave a lasting impression. It is an energetic, ancient city on the Vaigai River in the state of Tamil Nadu. Its skyline is dominated by the colourful gopurams (gateway towers) of Meenakshi Amman Temple. The temple is in the Dravidian style, covered in bright carvings of Hindu gods, and is a major pilgrimage site. Apparently millions attend the processions and ceremonies of the Chithirai Festival in April, celebrating Meenakshi and Vishnu.

We are too early for that, but we do come across a sizeable procession underway that evening when the sun goes down. Throngs of worshippers are out, paying their devotions to the numerous idols being 'put to bed' for the night – at least that is what's happening as far as we understand it. There is much chanting and a blaze of candles. Hundreds of folk line the colonnades of the temple looking on, while the procession goes around and around the outer circuit of the temple led by sixteen bare-chested men carrying a ceremonial bull. The noise is intense. Each time the crowd moves forward, it's more like a charge than a simple case of walking ahead. In this sea of Indian faces, many painted, many wearing elaborate headdresses, Tom – culture chameleon par excellence – blends in. *Not*. As I gaze across the multitude of worshippers, picking out Tom's white face and reddish whiskers is like playing the easiest game of *Where's Wally?* ever devised.

That evening we encounter a small group of Mancunian

A spare cave – the relative sanctuary of the 'guest room'. icky looking slightly nervous at the door's curity arrangements (a wheelbarrow). Meymand, Iran.

Netty outside the date palm oasis. Desert as far as the eye can see. Garmeh, Iran.

Welcome to India – a 5am arrival into Mumbai shakes even the most seasoned of travellers. Hicky still trying to get his head around the fact that the wheels have, literally, come off.

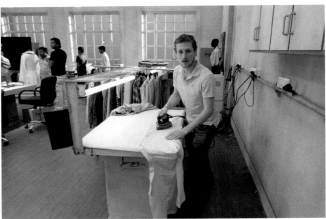

Badmaash (ironing) Company – becoming Bollywood stars, Mumbai, India.

Coast hopping – the start of the long drive south. Near Tarkali, north of Goa, India.

Christmas morning – opening stockings. Fort Aguada, India.

Hicky on the mic … audience of one. Fort Aguada, India.

Tom and friends – saluting the next generation. Tarkali Beach, India.

Skinheads – the transition from gentleman traveller to
England away fan. Gokarna, India.

Trekking the Western Ghats. Madikeri, India.

Biking/walking through the tea plantations. Munnar, India.

'I love India' – enough said, we both do. Near Madikeri.

Fulfilling our media obligations. Maharajah's palace, Bhitarkanika, India.

Air Guitar – the office. Eravikulam National Park, India.

The vibrant colours of the tribal lands. Orissa, India.

Acclimatising – a tea break en
route to Everest Base Camp.
Namache Bazaar, Nepal.

Glacial meltwaters – very cold,
honest! Gorak Shep, Nepal.

We're going where?! – Casual morning stroll over Gokyo Ri
glacier. No guide. Everest, Nepal.

Festival season – rocking out at Nepalese Glastonbury. Chakru.

Netty crossing the Tibetan plateau, 5,000m+ above sea level. Near Tingri.

gap-year travellers – all female – in our hotel. Romance having been decidedly lacking on our trip so far, I commit to dusting off the chat-up lines and start deploying my best small talk to rectify this state of affairs (backed up by the strongest local moonshine money can buy). Sadly on this occasion all concerned go a bit heavy on the local rat poison and the conversation becomes reminiscent of the dinner conversations on the ferry across the Caspian. The one shining ray of light is that I did find out the girls are heading to Thailand next and conclude that maybe this one has more to run. I cut my losses and get some rest, knowing that driving hungover in India is like trying to walk a tightrope with a rat dangling from your ear.

From Madurai, we reach the fishing village of Mamallapuram the next day. 250km in one hit. Again, there are fascinating things to see in the district: archaeological sites dating back to the 7th century, caves and temples of the Pallava dynasty. (My personal highlights are the five Rathas – huge carvings of elephants and temples cut out of a massive sheer granite wall, as fresh as the day they were first cut.) However, the town itself is regrettably squalid, and the heat and humidity intense. The drainage system is heavily polluted – the place is constructed over a swamp – and there are consequently swarms and swarms of mosquitoes.

Tom doesn't help matters. When we go out into the town to find some supper, Tom leaves the window of our hotel room open. 'It needs some air' are his famous last words. Upon return, we discover every insect within a mile has taken up residence in our cramped little room. An infestation of 'Boogen' (as we have come to call bugs of all descriptions) which we will come to rue by the morning. There follows a 'night of torment,' as I record in my journal. Wrapped up inside our sleeping bags with the drawstring pulled tight as it would go, the sound of mosquitos whining in for the attack – like a formation of tiny Second World War fighter planes that never run out of fuel – keeps us ducking and diving and very far from asleep. We give up at 4am and are driving out of Mamallapuram by 4:30am. Tom is the soul of contrition. This will not happen again, he promises.

Tom

A truly harrowing night and definitely my bad. We decide to put as much distance between us and Mamallapuram as possible. The road takes us straight through Chennai, slums and all. (There is no ring-road or bypass for the city.) Fettles are soon restored with a quick stop at a chai wallah – a man selling tea from a caddy on the side of the road. Beautiful stuff, this – unlike anything you can get anywhere else, even in the best hotels in India. Hicky is certain that the more dilapidated the cart, the better the tea. Certainly this neighbourhood is pretty shabby. But the chai is a delicious blend of tea, sugar and spices which we still talk about to this day.

We are crushing the mileage. The map indicates that we shouldn't be on a motorway but, continuing in its tradition of being consistently wrong, we happily whizz along asphalt the whole way. First to Vijayawada where we stop for a night, and then on to the coastal city of Vishakhpatnam, which reminds us of a rather tired old English seaside town. We drive a little further to – according to our trusty guidebook – 'the nicest beach in Andhra Pradesh' called Ro Beach. After the usual haggle, we manage to get a room for the night in an establishment resembling some sort of dilapidated Butlin's, complete with an empty swimming pool and faded brown plastic slide.

From here, we head inland, back up into the Eastern Ghats and Orissa, the poorest state in India. Orissa is not a common tourist destination so, struggling for places to go and things to see, we somehow find ourselves in the small 'spa hamlet' of Taptapani, for which even the *Lonely Planet* can't muster much enthusiasm. Apparently there is a local hot spring. However, it is something of a relief to leave National Highway 5 behind us and drive through some rural countryside again. The relative poverty of the region is evident as we drive from village to village. Folk live in huts and carry on what seems to be an entirely agrarian lifestyle. We drive over separated wheat sheaves, lain out on the road in large heaps to be threshed by passing cars and trucks for the grain to be collected later. Despite the little they have – from a passing car window at least – it seems basic, but a healthier, happier and more wholesome lifestyle than much of the squalor that people have to endure in a lot of the urban areas of India. Everyone up here is smiling. The colours of the women's saris are bright and gay. The countryside is charming. The children have space to play games and holler out at us as we drive past, waving. Many are naked. We pass an old man leaning on a staff, with leathery bare feet, an orange robe hitched up to his thighs and a long white triangular beard.

It feels like we have left the beaten track far behind us – albeit temporarily – something not easily done in this country. I snap away with my camera; in return the villagers stop and gape at the passing long wheelbase Land Rover manned by a pair of scruffy westerners, surely a rare sight in this neck of the woods.

In the government-run hotel in Taptapani we opt for the intriguingly named 'Roman style' room, which comes with a large tub supposedly supplied directly from the famous 'hot spring'. There's not a lot hot about it, in fact. But we enjoy the concept nevertheless. Even the public bath in the town was a bit of a mis-sell. Again, not what you could call a hot spa, just a tiled plunge pool filled with a lot of locals scrubbing themselves furiously. We hastily abandon whatever cleansing benefits are to be had here. Instead we go for a walk and are glad we do. Taptapani is set high in the Eastern Ghats. The hills and valleys are rich and green and lush. It is incredibly beautiful up here. And peaceful. Pleasant respite from the heat and humidity experienced so far up the east coast of India.

Upon our return, we discover two other English guests at the hotel – an older couple, Dave and Barbara, who are revisiting Taptapani having first been here back in 1971 when they travelled overland from London to Delhi. We are impressed that they have made it here; even in a car it's a long way off the tourist trail, let alone by the public transport they're using. We chat for a long while, enjoying their many tales of far-flung travel. They say they know a *bona fide* Maharajah who is restoring a decaying palace north-east of the city of Bhubaneswar.

'They'd love to meet you,' they tell us and say they're happy to put us in touch.

We still have some time to kill before reaching Kolkata (still referred to by everyone we met as Calcutta) so we agree that rubbing shoulders with Indian royalty is no bad way to do it. That decided, the following day, after we have moved on to the village of Rambha on the southern shores of Lake Chilika, Hicky has a reading day while I go for an amble around the place.

It proves to be one of my best days in India. As I'm walking along, a young man of about twenty falls in beside me on his bicycle. He introduces himself as Jan. His lips are stained and his cheeks bulging with the paan that he's chewing, but he's happy to chat away in faltering English. Before long he invites me to his village to see his home and meet his family. I hesitate for a moment but then think, why not? He hops on the central bar of his bicycle, I jump on the seat and off we go together. Under his direction and my pedal power we soon arrive at his hamlet with him hollering at the top of his voice to all and sundry to come and meet his pet foreigner, pointing at me over his shoulder. There followed much hand-shaking, taking of photos, tea-drinking with the family and good cheer, in addition to a short tour of his little village: the pond where he washes, even the field where he defecates – all commented on with boundless enthusiasm. He is so taken with his new friend that he accompanies me all the way back to the hotel, where I can only excuse myself finally with some lame story about Hicky being sick and my needing to tend to him. (Even then, this isn't the last I will see of him during our stay.) But I am grateful for an insight into Indian village life that I haven't yet experienced.

Hicky

Lake Chilika is meant to be a well-stocked lake of natural beauty. Personally, all I see is a muddy lake with not a lot to it and I'm not sorry when we move on to Bhubaneswar. We have rung ahead to the contact whom Dave and Barbara gave us – the now-fabled Mr Singh Dakh Kubhvi who will arrange our visit with the Maharajah. (His cousin, apparently.) He tells us on the phone that the Maharajah requires a couple of days' notice before our arrival, so he suggests we go to Puri, a nearby coastal town, first.

This proves a pleasant enough place with a stunning beach, and it provides a good base from which to visit the famous Sun Temple at Konark. This temple is thought to have been built by a king called Narasimhadeva I of the Eastern Ganga Dynasty around 1250 AD. Dedicated to the Hindu god Surya, what remains of the temple complex has the appearance of a one-hundred-foot-high chariot with immense wheels and horses, all carved from stone. A lot of it is in ruins now, but the structures and elements that survive are famed for their intricate artwork, iconography, and themes – particularly, it has to be said, its manifold and detailed depictions of the *Kama Sutra* and *mithunam* (more in the way of erotic ritual). We drift along with the other tourists, gawping in amazement at the reliefs twisted into various wild contortions. We read that *mithunam* – ritualised sexual union – is effective only when 'consecrated'. This means that the couple for the time being literally become divine: she is the goddess Shakti, he is the god Shiva. However, the Vedas warn that unless this spiritual transformation occurs, the union is carnal and therefore sinful.

It strikes us as a pretty fine line to tread. But if these carvings are anything to judge by, there have been plenty of Indian folk over the centuries game to take the chance. Possibly the less said about the depictions of bestiality the better.

Afterwards we go for a roam on the beach which, but for the litter strewn everywhere and the ordure lapping gently at the shoreline, would be a lovely spot. A local fisherman approaches us and before long he's talked

Tom into having fresh fish for dinner at his house up the beach. The area where he lives is very poor. Most people, he tells us, eke out a living by catching fish from the tiny wooden boats pulled up the sand. His house consists of a single room, with a small courtyard at the back, a tiny, thatched storeroom, the requisite TV and a Hindu shrine. One can't help feeling for him and his family of sixteen (father, four sons, three daughters, spouses and children). It must be a struggle to survive. The meal is simple but delicious. Grilled sardines, calamari, rice and boiled potatoes. Although Tom has to give me a dig in the ribs after they serve it up and I start to ask for cutlery.

'Hands only, Hickman,' he hisses under his breath.

From one extreme to the other. We rendezvous with Mr Singh Dakh (which I adapt to 'Singdog') in Bhubaneswar. He will be our guide for the palace visit. He is a big, brash man with a large goitre under his chin. It is only with some difficulty that he manages to climb aboard the Netster. He immediately announces that we will be having lunch in another palace.

'Don't worry – it is on the way to my cousin's palace,' he declares merrily.

'Who owns this other one then?' asks Tom.

'Also my cousin. She is my niece, in fact.'

For a man so well connected with royalty, Singdog is remarkably shabby. Not to mention fragrant in the close confines of Netty's interior.

Palace No. 1 (as we call it) must once have been a magnificent building. But today it's frankly a wreck. The young couple who greet us – Singdog's niece and her husband – are not at all what we expect. They live in only four rooms of this vast derelict pile, and her belief that she can have the place turned around and back to its former glory in under a year seems to us wildly optimistic – particularly as there is no sign of any building work going on at all. Still, we smile and make encouraging noises and are rewarded with a fine lunch eventually for which they will accept no money. It would appear we are their guests and not their clients, as we had assumed. They send us off with a gift of home-made pickle.

Singdog assures us that Palace No. 2 is an altogether grander affair. He's not wrong. Although still in need of a good deal of work (and money), Kanika Palace is considerably bigger and in much better condition. A large dirty white sprawl with dirty green shades curving over each window and a circular ornamental fountain at the front. Even in its shabby state, one can imagine the approach to this building could be impressive, except that the drive is merely a dusty track. This time there are at least builders labouring away when we arrive.

The Maharajah greets us himself, with garlands of flowers and a dab of dry red ochre on our foreheads. Then he shows us to our more than comfortable room. It turns out we won't be paying anything. We are to be his guests. Which is very gracious of him since he doesn't know us from Adam. He is a charming, affable, softly-spoken man in his late forties. He talks fluently and engagingly about his various estates and palaces, business ventures and responsibilities as king. After the two days we spend with him, he certainly appears to be the real deal. (As if it's for us to judge, but still.) He seems to command genuine respect and deference from those around him. His plan is to refurbish the palace and then convert it into a hotel. We certainly have a lot more faith that this will come to pass than the refurbishment at Palace No. 1 (and that the final result could be rather splendid).

Early in the morning, Singdog gives us a boat tour around the nearby wetlands called Bhitarkanika Wildlife Sanctuary. The object of the exercise is mainly to see crocodiles at home in the wild. (They live in these marshes where sweet and salt waters mingle, and which are more than a touch reminiscent of the Fens back home.) We do spy one large adult croc as we climb into the boat. After that it's only tiddlers. Nevertheless, Singdog is eager to point out other wildlife as well, at one point startling me with a sudden jab in the ribs.

'Look! Rrrrricky!' he cries. (Singdog finds my name unpronounceable.) He points up into one of the trees. 'Mon-key.'

This one will stay with us for the whole trip.

Back at Kanika Palace, we find ourselves unwittingly roped into an interview with the Orissa state newspaper, the *Bhubaneswar Star*. Apparently the lure of an audience with the King *and* two Englishmen in a Land Rover is too big a scoop to miss. The journalist assures us that there will be a double-page spread with photos in the Sunday magazine. We surmise that this has all been carefully arranged by the Maharajah to showcase his restoration project at Kanika Palace and we are only too happy to play along: we've answered so many questions about what we are doing and where we've been that it all trips off the tongue rather easily now. The Maharajah is only too enthusiastic about getting us some coverage. Which merely goes to show, I guess – even royalty needs a bit of shameless self-promotion now and then.

We never do see the article.

Tom
There is a lot of chat about the Black Hole of Calcutta on

the road north, which proves either ironic or prophetic on arrival, since at once we get horrifically lost on our way into the old imperial capital, thanks to our map and a bewilderingly complicated one-way system. Very scenic and all that, but the streets we are following get smaller and smaller and narrower and narrower and filled with more and more people and market stalls and animals and telephone cables and washing lines and awnings and goodness knows what else until we are well and truly stuck. We are hemmed in by the noise of hawkers yelling, the smells emanating from cooking pots, gutters and sacks of spices, and the swelter of this sprawling city. Crowds of people swarm around the car, probably wondering what on earth these pale-faced clowns are doing trying to drive a long wheelbase Land Rover down a pedestrian street in central Calcutta.

Still, once you're in there's no chance of backing out the way you have come so we push on. I am driving at snail's pace and Hicky is alternately standing on the mounting step outside or crouched on the roof, waving aside man and beast, lifting up washing lines, electrical cables and low-hanging awnings over Netty's windscreen and roof rack like an explorer chopping leaves in a jungle. Eventually, with much persistence and a bit of luck, we pop out into something like a proper thoroughfare and away we go again.

We are heading for the home of our contacts, the Kumars. Sunita and Naresh are very old friends of my parents who I have met over the years in London and also in Delhi on my prior trip to India. They will kindly be hosting us for the duration of our stay in Calcutta. We arrive here on February 23rd and will stay until March 11th. The reason for our lengthy sojourn is that we have arranged to do some volunteer work at Mother Teresa's Home of the Destitute and Dying. Most of the overland expeditions that we have read about at some point do something to 'give back'. This is our attempt to do the same. The irony, of course, is that by the end of our time in Calcutta we will feel like we have received far more than we could ever have given in return.

The Kumars live in a beautifully appointed and spacious apartment in the centre of Calcutta, though it's barely two miles – but a world – away from the slums where Mother Teresa ministered to the poor at the Mother House of the Missionaries of Charity. They are rather elderly now – Naresh is north of ninety – but you'll never meet a more beautiful, inspiring, welcoming and interesting couple. We are genuinely blessed to have been able to spend some time with them. We see in their family photos that Sunita was a rare beauty in her younger days, and she is still very captivating with blown-back grey hair and very wise, dark, kind eyes. She is an artist. And for nearly fifty years she has been a volunteer worker for Mother Teresa's Missionaries of Charity, but more importantly Mother Teresa's friend, confidante, *de facto* spokeswoman and, more unusually, her painter. (She once had an exhibition of her paintings of Mother Teresa in London. And more recently, she has even designed saris for Hermès.)

Naresh Kumar was, for a long time, an international tennis star. He played at Wimbledon no fewer than twenty times, competing every year from 1949 to 1969. Since his sporting retirement he's become an industrialist, and a hugely successful one, too. He stands straight as a spear, looks you dead in the eye, and has a warm smile made mischievous by his two bushy eyebrows, his grey brush of a moustache and the twinkle in his eye.

We are to discover over the coming days that he is also a storyteller par excellence. Indeed, they both are.

I record in my journal that they are 'a truly amazing pair of individuals' and that it is hard to do them justice with my paltry writing skills and lack of patience. Perhaps it's enough to say that both Hicky and I soon agreed they had lived and continue to live inspiring lives. We are deeply grateful to have had the privilege of getting to know them.

Hicky

To give you a flavour of Naresh's storytelling – his conversation ranges from recounting his escapades against Rod Laver on the tennis court, to dinners with the same in the Dorchester, through to his heart-wringing description of Sunita's battle against a rare form of cancer, for which she was treated in Paris for seven months. Naresh stayed at her bedside the whole time or else walked the streets praying for her cure. (Which thankfully did come about.) From the emotional to the ridiculous, he also brings alive Calcutta with stories from the street, such as the one about a store-keeper who drew a line on the dusty road, announcing that any person who crossed the line would think they were burning to death and that the hallucination would never stop unless they first gave the store-keeper a rupee. Everyone ridiculed the store-keeper for a fool and a charlatan until an English army officer strode boldly across the line and immediately began tearing at his clothes as if he was on fire, until – in his agony – he managed to hand over a rupee, whereupon the pain stopped. After that the onlookers naturally all paid up. 'But of course,' smiles Naresh, 'the English officer was in on the act.'

Sunita, on the other hand, is a fount of stories about her years working with Mother Teresa, which have made her witness to almost innumerable instances of miraculous healing, divine provision and answers to prayer. Up till now I would consider myself pretty cynical about this sort of thing. But after hearing story after story from Sunita, it becomes very hard to deny the miraculous occurrences that seemed to surround the life of Mother Teresa. It's either that or countless cases of coincidence, the odds of which are too improbable to countenance – and the string of coincidences becomes almost harder to accept than some sort of intervention by a higher power. I'll give you one example. Sunita tells us that she is friends with the famous Indian cricketer, Kapil Dev. He and his wife Romi had been married since 1980, but despite years of trying, they remained childless. They had an opportunity to meet Mother Teresa in private. She prayed for them and laid hands on his wife's head and stomach. Within three months of this prayer, she became pregnant.

Another story she tells us is, in fact, one that was cited in the evidence presented to the Vatican in support of Mother Teresa's canonisation: a woman in Bengal suffering from a large tumefaction of about sixteen centimetres in her abdomen (she was unable to undergo an operation because she also suffered from tuberculosis) went to mass on the one-year anniversary of Mother Teresa's death. There, she 'saw' a ray of light emit from a picture of Mother Teresa. Encouraged, the woman went forward for prayer and one of the Missionaries of Charity Sisters took a medal of the Virgin Mary which had touched directly the body of Mother Teresa at her funeral and tied it to the suffering woman's belly. The Sister then prayed a very simple prayer asking for Mother Teresa to help the woman. The medical reports show that eight hours later, the tumour had completely disappeared, a fact attested to by eleven doctors (only two of whom were Catholic). The doctors concluded that there was no medical explanation as to how the tumour had disappeared so quickly.

Sunita is full of such stories. It's little wonder that the Vatican summoned her to Rome as one of the witnesses of Mother Teresa's life when they were considering the case for raising her to sainthood. Since the Mother was indeed canonised in 2016, I guess they believed her.

It takes us two days to register at the Home of the Destitute and Dying in the district of Kalighat. This is the original house which Mother Teresa set up to provide care for the dying amongst the poorest of the poor of the city. We quickly discover that we are merely two of a large number of other volunteers hailing from all over the world who have come to offer their time and energy, and it quickly becomes clear to us that there are far more volunteers than can be usefully employed. For this reason, when one of the Sisters asks for two volunteers to work in the afternoons on another site, we stick our hands up (ever game for something new). This other site turns out to be in a district called Daya Dan – a home for disabled and mentally challenged children. So for the next three weeks we will be serving in the Kalighat house in the mornings and the Daya Dan house during the afternoons.

It proves to be an altogether extraordinary experience. Each day we would rise early and walk the two miles from the Kumars' apartment through the southern ghettos of Kolkata to the Kalighat. Once through the door, each volunteer leaves behind him background, ego, everything about his other life. Each person is treated simply on the basis of the things they do in the house and the personality that they present – whether that's friendly, engaged, remote, distressed, humble, disdainful, whatever. It's up to you. My time there teaches me many things, perhaps most evident are tolerance, patience and humility. It is humbling to see so many people have come to this place to serve these unfortunates who are in such a wretched condition. I haven't ever seen a dead body up to this point – possibly an indication of having lived a sheltered life, but that's simply the way it is. Yet the dignity which the Sisters and volunteers strive to give the sick and the dying cannot fail to impact even the stoniest of hearts. We are only doing basic tasks – helping in the kitchen, cleaning bed sheets, preparing food, cleaning dishes, cleaning up around the house – but they become almost exhilarating.

I am particularly struck by some of the other volunteers at the Kalighat house. Hearing their stories and why they have come here is inspiring. I make some good friendships over the course of our time at the house. Most of them are Christians, as of course is the whole operation set up by Mother Teresa. I wouldn't call myself religious, although I'm not hostile to faith as some can be. But it is certainly striking to meet people so motivated by their faith that they come all the way to Kolkata to serve. There is Charles, a hospice nurse from New York, who has a cheeky sense of humour and not a bad bone in his body. A few other young men, hardly more than kids really, just out of high school in Chicago, who are always laughing and provide much amusement for the rest of us. Then there is Sergio, a screenwriter and restaurateur from Madrid, who commits to coming here for three weeks of every year, just to interact with people outside of his world and to help out the disadvantaged.

'It feels like we are here to help them,' he says one morning. 'But really it's them who are helping us. I spend my life around people interested only in serving themselves. When I'm here, it reminds me that life is not all about me.'

Being around people who don't just talk about doing good but actually get on and do it, somehow starts to rub off on one, to open one's eyes to what is possible. Even though there are dozens of us at the house – too many – I find I can't help but dream of what humanity could be. The basic values of loving each other, helping people worse off than yourself, affording people dignity whatever wretched state life has reduced them to – these are great gifts to take away from my time among the volunteers, the Sisters, and those who come to this house in need and will never leave it.

The afternoon work is a little different. At the home for disabled and mentally challenged children, we are charged with tutoring a couple of kids for two hours, and then playing with a classroom of children for a further hour. I am put with a boy called Justice – at thirteen the oldest of the group, though he is probably the most severely mentally handicapped as well. They give me various exercises to do with him. Basic counting, word recognition, things like that. Very simple, really. There is endless repetition, distraction, or simple failure to comprehend. After the first day, I find myself wondering how on earth I am going to cope with three weeks of this. But the strange thing is that … I do. Ordinarily I would lose my patience in a heartbeat. Instead I fall into Justice's rhythm of doing things and by the end of our time together, I feel a genuine bond to him and to the other kids – Bernard, Rakesh, Rahul. They are always smiling, always laughing. That's infectious.

I'll certainly never forget them.

There are only two niggles in my mind about the whole experience. The first has to do with that bond I just mentioned. Over our three weeks, both Tom and I become very close to the children. We do wonder about the effect on them of an endless series of volunteers dropping into their lives, creating similar bonds, only to leave again so soon. Is that entirely fair on the children? I don't know. Maybe they are more inured to it than I give them credit for. Maybe they don't even notice.

The second niggle is how easy it is for us to dip in and out of the abject poverty and suffering we witness in the Kalighat house. On a few of the days, between our morning and afternoon sessions, we have lunch at the Tollygunge Club as guests of the Kumars' forty-year-old son, Arjun. The Tollygunge is the only country club of its kind in India and rates itself as among the top twenty clubs in the world. It has more than a whiff of the old colonial life of privilege about it. Here we enjoy delicious food, ice-cold beers, cocktails; we play tennis, we swim. Self-evidently this is a world away from what is going on in either of the houses where we are working. In the evenings – again courtesy of Arjun's hospitality – there are parties and dinners and exclusive nightclubs, enough champagne to float a battleship and endless exotic feasts (mainly comprising of every kind of curry under the sun). This is all great fun and very welcome. But the contrast is more than striking. I suppose the question is what does one learn from this? Should we feel guilty because of all we have? Or simply grateful that we are not locked into that other world of suffering? How should we make sense of that? After all, we can jump in our car and leave it all behind us whenever we want.

At the very least, it will be difficult to take the good things in my life for granted ever again. Indeed I hope I will not.

Tom

Despite our warm welcome in the bosom of the Kumars' home, I've been feeling pretty low for some days leading up to our arrival in Calcutta. I suppose it is for this reason that my experience of the Kalighat house and the droves of volunteers is a bit different to Hicky's. I find myself not wanting to interact with the other volunteers once we have registered and got our bearings. Also, rightly or wrongly, I sense a division of status between those volunteers who care for the patients and those who carry out the support tasks. We avoid the volunteer breakfast – ostensibly to ensure we find ourselves something useful to do before all the jobs of any substance are gone – but even at lunchtime I hide away in a corner and write postcards by myself in order to avoid having to engage with all the people whom Hicky is enjoying so much.

To his credit, he does notice this and at one point comes over and asks me what's up. He says he can't read me at all and can't understand why I don't want to get to know the others in the group. I can't really give him an explanation, but assure him it's nothing to do with him. The fact that my best friend and travelling companion can't read me does sort of snap me out of myself, though. And looking back, I wonder whether my low mood may be more attributable to a sudden deterioration in my health that is brewing – but more of that in a moment.

At the Kalighat house, my reticence and need for isolation (and, perversely, a sense of being cut out of the clique of important jobs) somehow impels me to get involved with the most challenging (read: distasteful) tasks I can find. The work in the house is divided more or less into two. As it were, front of house and backstage. In the back, the jobs are all cleaning, washing clothes, hanging clothes, washing dishes, maintenance and food preparation/service etc. In the front, the work is caring for the patients who come into the house either sick or dying. This means assisting the nurses/Sisters in duties such as cleaning and dressing wounds, but also carrying out other basic tasks: emptying bedpans or urine flasks, distributing water to patients, massaging aching backs and limbs, even scratching some of them.

Although no one has told me to get involved in the 'front of house' work, I take it upon myself to find a way and discover that simply by walking through the dormitory where the patients are lying, invariably someone calls out to you for help and you become immediately involved.

The first time I do this I'm called upon to change someone's soiled pyjamas. Unpleasant stuff, to be sure, but this is the reality of it. I am glad for the challenge and I prefer this to sitting upstairs. As you would expect, the patients are mostly in a very sorry state, some horrifically so. And a lot of them are emaciated beyond anything that I at least have witnessed before. Seeing corpses and the dead being carried out wrapped in a sheet becomes an everyday experience here.

On another occasion, I have to massage the shoulders of a man with one of the most grisly wounds I've ever seen – a huge abscess eating away at the poor man's perineum (the small area between his genitals and his anus). I get to know this Patient #21 quite well. It's worth quoting direct from my journal at this point:

Despite [his horrific ailment] he had a very kind face, immaculate manners and I never heard him utter a peep when the Italian nurse was cleaning his wound. The first time I gave him a massage the doctor came to the bed and told him that he was going to get surgery. This was great news and would eventually see him back on his feet. The second time I massaged him he went to take my hand in gratitude as I finished. Thanking me profusely he grabbed my arm with both hands. All of a sudden I felt the grip tighten and his face, bit by bit, lost its shape as he dissolved into silent but racking sobs. Holding his upper arm and talking as calmly as I could I told him not to worry, that the doctor had promised him surgery and all would be well. After no more than thirty seconds the tears had gone and the serene face was back in position. I can't properly describe the force of will it must have taken to control so quickly emotions which had obviously come from such a deep place. In my opinion the tears were largely fear and loneliness. These he had kept bottled up but when shown a little kindness, his emotions – which no doubt had been desperately looking for a way of showing themselves – forced their way to the surface. It seemed to me a perfect example of what Mother Teresa was all about. Showing a bit of love to those that have none. The fact that it was me was irrelevant and if I had not been walking past his bed he would have asked the next volunteer. I was just lucky to see this effect in action as it was a valuable lesson to learn.

After that experience, it is especially distressing to learn the next day that the money for Patient #21's operation has fallen through. The nurse and the resident chaplain vehemently argue the case on his behalf but the doctor says his hands are tied. When I discover that the amount needed to fund the operation is R70,000 (roughly £1,000) this becomes something of a moral dilemma (or at least a question) for me over the course of my day off. So much so that I ring my bank manager to find out whether my account is in any fit state to donate the necessary funds. As it happens, when I return on the Friday, both Patient #21 and my dilemma have gone: the operation is going ahead after all.

My desire to be thrown in at the deep end is soon more than fulfilled by a quirk in the holiday rota. One of the regular nurses has gone on holiday and, short of professional help, Charles the hospice worker from New York has been asked to fill in. Honestly, I didn't know people like Charles exist. I have never met such an open, positive, grateful and friendly man in all my life. I was drafted in as his assistant and we spent the next few days cleaning and dressing the various wounds that found their way, often several weeks after the accident, into the Kalighat house. I will spare the details here but suffice to say that the first order of business, invariably, was to remove the infestations of maggots which gave these terrible injuries the illusion that they were alive, swollen seams of pulsating flesh. My journal simply says, 'While working with Charles I saw the most horrific things of my life so far. There is no need to recount them here. They are burnt into my memory for life.'

Hicky has already mentioned his experiences at Daya Dan and mine are rather similar. My very first encounter upon entering the house involves a small boy tugging obstinately at my arms asking to be picked up. When I oblige him and perch him on my hip, this is the moment he chooses to wet himself, soaking me at the same time. My main charge, however, is a boy called Rakesh. He can't walk so I have to carry him upstairs to the tiny cubicle where, over the next two weeks, I help him study. Rakesh has an impressively short attention span. (He asks me ten times a session what the same nail sticking out of the wall is.) He is also highly susceptible to any change in the tone of my voice. Nevertheless, I have many funny moments teaching him, and making him laugh is a real treat as it is always accompanied by his beaming and guileless smile.

There is another slightly younger boy called Bernard whom I get to look after with Hicky during group playtime. He doesn't have the use of his legs either. One afternoon I have to take him to the loo. However, not knowing how to help him given his permanently crossed legs, I prop him on the loo and go to tell a Sister that we need help. But by the time she arrives it's too late; Bernard has peed all over himself. He laughs his head off at this. I later note in my journal: 'I could certainly do with a bit more of that sort of attitude in my life.'

Perhaps we all could.

As I touched on earlier, whatever is wrong with my stomach has been getting worse recently. Given our relatively stable situation staying with the Kumars, I decide to sort this out once and for all and ask them to recommend a doctor. Sunita kindly books me an appointment for Monday morning. Over the weekend my stomach gets steadily worse so I am relieved when Monday morning at last comes. Sunita packs me off with one of their drivers to a nearby hospital for my appointment. However, as I arrive, I am feeling horrendous and soon have to rush to the bathroom, thinking I am about to vomit. I'm not really sure what happens next. At the time I wonder whether I am hallucinating. All I can remember is a sensation that everything is rising in my body, rushing towards my head where it will eventually erupt out of the top of my skull. I vaguely remember my hands rising to my head, as I burst out of the bathroom and stagger down the corridor, bouncing off the walls like the town drunk. Finally, I tumble through the swing-doors into the hospital waiting room and collapse unconscious into the arms of Sunita's driver. The poor man nearly has a fit himself, thinking he's just killed the Kumars' English guest.

Unsurprisingly I am seen by a doctor in short order after this little performance and he quickly diagnoses my condition as acute gastritis, recommending that I stay in hospital for another two days on a drip. This is the last thing I want to do. Instead I make every excuse under the sun to return home to the Kumars, which I figure will be a much more comfortable convalescence than anything I would get in hospital. In the face of my protestations, they let me go, despite the fact that I faint yet again when giving a blood sample.

Over the next two days my condition does improve, and by the time I am back on my feet, we have already overrun our scheduled stay. It's time to head for Nepal.

We bid farewell to our friends, our experiences here etched on our memories and hearts, and perhaps not quite the same men who arrived in Kolkata three weeks before.

Now we turn our noses to the north and set a course for the roof of the world.

EIGHT

To the Roof of the World

Hicky

The culmination of India is to be the city Varanasi. The climax and the totem of everything that we find good and bad about the country. In some ways it is the perfect place from which to draw a line under everything that we have experienced and launch our escape into Nepal and the mighty Himalayas to the north-west.

It's a two-day drive from Calcutta to Varanasi, more or less to the west along a motorway. We break the journey with a stopover at Bodhgaya – arguably the most important site in the Buddhist religion. This is where Gautama Buddha attained enlightenment sitting under a tree. The tree became known as the Bodhi Tree. (*Bodhi* meaning Enlightenment.) There is still a tree to visit and gawp at – even sit under if you like (apparently a descendant of the original tree which Buddha sat under two and a half thousand years ago). It's been a place of pilgrimage from the days of the Buddha's earliest disciples.

Alas, and perhaps predictably, when the two of us lurk under the Bodhi Tree's sacred branches, we attain … precisely nothing.

'Our pilgrimage towards Enlightenment demands a longer road,' intones Tom when we climb back in Netty.

I consider this for a few moments. 'Well, I do feel really bad about the dog.' This, referring to the feral one I ran over on the motorway the day before. It came out of nowhere. No time to swerve. Terrible tragedy, officer. (You know the drill.) 'Does that count?'

'It's a start, I s'pose.'

From the outset Varanasi is intense.

Finding our way into the city is similar to our entry into Calcutta only worse; the roads seem to close in even narrower and are even more over-crowded, creating a stinking sweltering smoking bright and noisy assault on all the senses. It takes us another couple of hours after reaching the city to find the hotel we have decided to stay in.

I record in my journal that there is simply no empty space in this city. Varanasi sprawls along the right hand (southern) bank of the Ganges River, almost toppling right into it down the miles and miles of ghats (embankments stepped in stone that lead down into the water) which line its course. The other river bank is completely open and undeveloped. The city leaves that side for the feral dogs which roam its length scavenging for a free meal. (More on that later.)

But even before we walk down to the river, just wandering through the back streets and alleys is an overwhelming experience. Throngs of vendors clog the cramped, dark streets. The air is pungent with spices and food-stalls, smoke from wood fires, exhaust fumes, sweat and sewage, dust and animal dung.

Varanasi is the place Hindus come to die, thanks to the belief that cremation in the holy Ganges River guarantees the Hindu his salvation. Certainly the city abounds with dead bodies and the stacks and stacks of firewood needed to burn them. Varanasi is a major religious hub – the holiest of the seven sacred cities. Pilgrims come here to wash in the holy waters of Mother Ganga and, if they are fortunate, their relatives will burn their bodies on the ghats above the river and scatter their ashes on its surface.

The bodies are one of the first things we notice, wrapped in orange sheets, carried around the streets on wooden stretchers on their way to the cremation sites along the ghats, borne up by processions of their relatives dressed in equally colourful attire amid a clamour of musical accompaniment (mainly drums). Indeed, the whole place is a blast of colour and noise – with saris of every shade and style, turbans of red or white or yellow or orange, holy men daubed in white paint, shouts and chanting and singing and weeping and wailing.

Tom
Extraordinary as it is to take all this in, we discover that the best way to observe is from a boat on the river itself. So on the second day, we find ourselves a likely-looking 'Boat Phil', take up position in his little rowing boat and float along the Ganges feasting on all we can see. The cremations are one thing, but perhaps more remarkable is the range of life that is lived out along the ghats. People washing clothes, bathing themselves, relieving themselves, selling goods and food, acting out all kinds of ritual ablutions from several different faiths, or transporting stuff up and down the river in the boats which swarm along the bank. And of course the river itself is full of visitors like us bobbing around in a sprawling flotilla, gawping at it all and taking photos.

Boat Phil does his best to impress quite how holy are the waters of Mother Ganga. He even scoops up some in his hand and drinks it, then encourages us to do the same.

'Fancy a drop?' I ask Hicky.

'Over my dead body.'

'It probably would be.' Experts estimate that more than 3,000 million litres of untreated sewage are pumped into the Ganges every day from the towns and cities upstream of Varanasi. By the time the water reaches Varanasi itself, whose untreated sewage also goes straight into the river, the Ganges has become the most polluted river in the world.

We forego Boat Phil's invitation. And, as if we needed any assurance of the wisdom of that decision, a few moments later he pulls us across the river near the left bank where he points out four or five feral dogs tearing at something beached in the mud at the water's edge. As we draw closer the stench attains a level of putrescence I've never known. We soon discover why. The 'something beached in the mud' is in fact a badly mauled (and badly wrapped) dead body. Boat Phil tells us that there are five types of pilgrims who cannot be burned on the ghat pyres. These unfortunates are: babies; pregnant women; lepers; sadhus (holy men); and those bitten by a cobra. Instead these folk are wrapped in linen burial shrouds, together with some fairly hefty weights, and dropped into the middle of the river, the hope being that the weights will keep them submerged. Of course, as they rot, some bodies break free from their watery restraints and float to the surface, there to become the food of the packs of feral dogs that roam the far river bank.

Boat Phil asks us if we want to go closer and to our

mutual shame we both nod. It could just be the falling light, but it seems to me that Hicky has turned distinctly grey of hue as all this is explained, to the accompaniment of the dogs growling and grinding and gulping not thirty feet away.

As dusk turns to night, we return to the near bank where the ghats are lit up in earnest with the cremation pyres and the candles sent floating down the river.

For all the visual and spiritual intoxication of the place, which is impressive, after a couple of days here we begin to feel that it is becoming oppressive, too. On the last day, Hicky refuses to go out, electing instead to confine himself to the hotel room and watch endless episodes of *Curb Your Enthusiasm* (an American sitcom) on his computer. I have some sympathy for him. Everyone has their sensory overload point and we have pretty much reached ours. It is time to depart India and head for clearer air.

Hicky

It is a relief to leave behind the cramped confines of Varanasi, in many ways the culmination of our time in India and all that it represents, and instead set Netty on a course for the mountains. From the Ganges valley we head north to Gorakhpur and then turn north-east towards the border town of Raxaul, surely one of the most miserable places we have yet to pass through.

For a long section of the drive leading up to the Nepalese border, the landscape flattens out into a featureless plain, drab and joyless, and yet knowing that the Himalayas lie somewhere ahead, one tingles with anticipation for the huge walls of rock that will soon break out of the surface and rise up in front of us.

But even at the border crossing, this still lies ahead. Raxaul is a filthy place – literally – since motorists crossing the border take the opportunity to divest their vehicles of every piece of litter on board. No one bothers to clear it up. For me, it amounts to nothing better than a dustbowl of hawkers, decaying buildings and unrest. In our haste to be away from there, we somehow fail to receive the necessary exit stamp from India, or even notice the border post at all as it is innocuous beyond belief. Thus, at the Nepalese entry point we are sent back to India one last time to endure some protracted customs procedures. This feels familiar – you'll remember our Moldovan/Transnistrian border crossing debacle – although we do manage to get through without paying any *baksheesh*.

We are soon speeding into Nepal. With every passing mile, one feels the air clearing, as well as the landscape. The roadside litter ceases; the shanty towns fall behind in the rear-view mirror.

We have been warned that when the road at last rises up and out of the haze and the first of the Himalayas begin to emerge, we will be shocked. We are a little sceptical, as usual. But when the moment comes and we crest a smaller row of hills somewhere near the town of Daman, we have to pull over. Above us, almost magically floating in the clear abyss of sky, are the peaks and ridges of the Mahabharat Range. In the middle distance are the front rank of mountains that will climb higher and higher up to the highest peak of all, Mount Everest, or Sagarmatha as it is known in Nepalese.

For now, however, even the scale of these first peaks are humbling enough. We pull on our jumpers for the first time in months. The road begins to wind through increasingly fertile country. We are back in the land of

the most basic agrarian subsistence. It is notable that
the labourers in the small, terraced field are all women,
hoeing away with wooden tools, barefoot and dressed in
bright red clothing, or grinding their way uphill toting
giant sacks of what look like dead leaves on their backs.
One wonders what all the men are doing.

We receive at least a partial answer to that mystery
on our drive onwards from Daman. Rounding a corner,
we are brought to a sudden stop by a collection of men
chopping up a pine tree that has fallen in the middle of
the road. We squeeze Netty through the gap, inhaling
the fragrant scent of pine sap wafting in through the
open windows. A very pleasant way to blow away the last
vestiges of the more doubtful aromas of Varanasi.

Over each crest the mountains ahead only seem to grow
more immense. We are loving the clean air, the bright
clear skies, green mountains, the astonishing beauty of it
all, following the hundreds of hairpin bends ever higher
until at last we reach our immediate destination: the city
of Kathmandu.

It's another confused arrival. The ancient streets, clearly
not designed for long wheelbase Land Rovers, prove
more than a match for Netty. It doesn't help that we miss
a turning. We instantly make ourselves rather unpopular
by blocking one of the tiny streets and causing a huge tail
back, stirring up the ire of the normally peaceable local
populace far more than we would have liked. Still, after
a nineteen-point turn – in the style of Austin Powers – I
manage to extricate us from our bottleneck.

We have a contact in Kathmandu, one of mine this
time. His name is Dr Chiran Thapa. He is a former
Prime Minister of Nepal, a good friend of my father, and
perhaps the first man to walk into the chambers of the

Narayanhity Royal Palace after Prince Dipendra of Nepal went on the rampage, massacring ten members of his own family, this in 2001. All, allegedly, over a marriage dispute.

Chiran is rather busy, owing to the death of a more recent Prime Minister and the ceremonial demands that this places on him. However, he has very kindly organised the hotel for us, as well as found us a place to keep Netty while we explore Kathmandu and, more to the point, while we plan and execute our own hiking adventure: to reach Everest Base Camp.

Tom

We take a couple of days to get organised, enjoying the contrasts between Kathmandu and the India we have left behind. Kathmandu feels like an international city – you can play pool, drink beer, eat pizza, and even happen upon the most delicious tiramisu I've ever eaten. But the backdrop is sensational, too. The temple spires, the rather charming architecture of the ordinary houses, with their wooden window casings and shadowy eaves overhanging the streets, rather in the manner of Tudor times in England or even Florence today. Then there are the grander places like Durbar Square with its multi-tiered wooden temples, in one of which the only living 'goddess' resides. (Apparently spending a night in a dark room with a collection of severed buffalo heads without crying was one of the proofs of her divinity.) Or Monkey Temple with its white dome and giant golden stupa, or the big royal palaces that rise up like enormous wedding cakes, their walls red, their roofs golden against the far-off white peaks of the Himalayas.

Whilst casting an eye around us, our main objective

is to equip ourselves for the coming ordeal of our hike. Perhaps ill-advisedly, but certainly in keeping with our 'winging it' approach, we opt for the cheapest kit we can find, which we may yet come to regret. We have decided we don't need a proper guide or sherpas, both of which we have been advised to take and go ahead and book a flight to the little town of Lukla, the launch point for any hike heading towards Everest Base Camp (and beyond). Hickman has read somewhere that creating specific roles for team members encourages morale. As a result, I have been anointed team medic whilst he has christened himself head of communications. No doubt that will make up for the lack of professional support and so, after all this very strenuous preparation, we deem ourselves ready for whatever the world's largest mountain range can throw at us.

Streamlining our kit has not been a notable strength of ours so far on this trip and our backpacks rather prove the point. They weigh in at around twenty-two kilos each – a fair amount to heft up to where the air is only 'wafer-thin'. But in fact we don't even get that far before they start becoming tiresome.

It seems our flight to Lukla is grounded. (Something, we are told, that happens often. It is one of the most dangerous runways in the world.) Despite crystal-clear skies in Kathmandu, the weather has closed in around Lukla, at least sufficient to cancel all flights. So we wait and we wait. First one day, then a second, towards the end of which Hickman, fed up with lugging his enormous backpack to the airport and then back to our increasingly surprised hotel, tables the idea of commandeering a helicopter to get us there instead. (Not such an extravagant idea since their greatly reduced approach speed means that helicopters will be the first aircraft allowed to take off when the weather clears.) Perhaps, he argues, we can offset our savings on buying decent gear against the $350 this would cost each of us. I am half-convinced. On day three of our wait, however, he loses his rag.

'That's it!' he thunders. 'I don't care how much it costs. We're taking the helicopter. I'm paying.'

Which is extremely kind of him. Only two hours later we are taking off and are treated to a delightful flight over the hills to get us up to Lukla. And indeed the expense proves to be a fantastic decision since we are the first to arrive of the next wave of delayed hikers and thus the first to set out from there towards Namche Bazar, with a three-day gap between us and the last people ahead of us. Thanks to this, we find ourselves hiking in splendid isolation on a route which others have said can be a bit of a thoroughfare.

We shoulder our packs ready to leave, Hicky sporting his Norfolk flat cap as usual.

'Hang on a sec,' he says, and walks over to a nearby tree from which he rips off a branch and strips it down into something resembling a walking stick. 'Never go for a walk without a good stick,' he declares.

I have my doubts that this will help him in any way at all, but he seems happy and off we go.

We trek to a village going by the satisfying name of Phakding which at 2,610m above sea level is actually two hundred metres lower than Lukla airport. There we take a room in the first guest house we come across.

Hicky

This first day is something of a false dawn. My legs feel dead as the path heads straight up into the hills.

I am panting. But then, suddenly, we are treated to a mouth-watering tidbit: our first glimpse of Everest. This stems the pain, albeit only briefly, although it's not enough to stem the dread that this plucky pair of Englishmen may have winged it a bridge too far. With each step the packs on our backs feel more and more like concrete. We have been told that the hike on the second day to the town of Namche Bazar is about six or seven hours of walking. We take this long and possibly longer, but by now the bad weather has cleared and the views are staggering. We are also staggering; although we do somehow make it into the town, with jelly legs and light heads, utterly exhausted.

The altitude starts to hit our bodies at this point. My head is pounding; I'm short of breath. Namche Bazar sits at 3,420m above sea level. In other words, high enough that altitude sickness becomes a serious issue. For this reason, most hikers spend a couple of days in Namche acclimatising. After a late lunch we collapse onto the beds we have found. As we relax, watching more and more folks come in, on the one hand we feel put to shame by the sherpa porters who are weighed down with far more gear than we're lugging. On the other, we see no other foreign trekkers carrying their own packs, save for a couple of (rather impressive) women.

We have no guide, but we do follow the advice of our guidebook, which says that in order to acclimatise properly to the rising altitude and depleting oxygen, we should climb no more than four hundred vertical metres each day. In addition to that, we should climb higher than wherever we intend to sleep on each day in order to give us even half a chance of a decent night's sleep at this altitude. We stick to these rules of thumb religiously.

The following day we do a round trip hike of six hours or so – starting and ending in Namche Bazar and gloriously free of backpacks. The mountains are extraordinary; the sky clear and bright and we appear to have the place completely to ourselves. We both agree that, high as expectations have been, the reality of these mountains surpasses even one's wildest imaginings. We trek along shaded paths under pine forests, the air heady with the scent of pine needles. Tom tells me he has caught sight of a 'Himalayan pheasant'. As Norfolk stalwarts, this excites us perhaps more than it would your average hiker.

The next leg, a less popular route up and over some peaks towards a small guest house called Phortse Thang, takes us over 4,000m, and affords us a glimpse at village life on the roof of the world. One man working his ox and plough up and down his front garden; along the dusty street a group of elderly women with deeply lined faces spinning prayer beads and drums, chanting 'Om Mare Padre Om'. (Or something like it.) The last part of the trek plunged steeply down from a great height to our destination for the day in Phortse Thang (at 3,680m).

Perhaps foolishly – no, *definitely* foolishly – rather than pay R300 per person (equivalent to five quid) for a hot bucket of water in the guest house, we opt for a tops-and-tails dip in the glacial river running just below the lodge. Tom looks like the most wretched of creatures cowering in this stream. He is beyond speech. His ribcage seems to go into spasm, and when he comes up after dunking a second time to wash off his soap, he can't speak for nearly half a minute.

I, on the other hand, can say plenty – mostly very loud and in terms decidedly unedifying for any trekkers who happen to be within earshot.

Tom

The Himalayan serenity is truly unique. Nevertheless, I am finding the whole experience rather like the curate's egg. The good parts are self-evident. The bad parts, less so. As we climb higher, the altitude imposes on us much shorter distances each day. So much so that the day becomes mostly filled with sitting about in the hiking lodges with no electricity, heating or lighting, waiting for night to fall. For this reason, I am in favour of taking our time on the walks, spinning them out, making the most of the time in the extraordinary surroundings. Hicky, on the other hand, seems determined to turn every hike into a relentless physical and mental battle, pushing on to the point of exhaustion at all times. Unfortunately my own competitive nature refuses to allow me to let him disappear into the distance whilst I trundle along at my own speed. Challenge thrown down. Challenge accepted.

We continue in this vein – slogging our way uphill, biting off little pieces each day – up past 4,000m and then soaring over the infamous Cho La Pass, standing at some 5,420m above sea level. By now, there's no time to dwell on wasted hours. Everything is a physical struggle, everything a physical achievement. Everything is breath-takingly beautiful and bewilderingly huge. The days start with blazing sunshine and brilliant skies and usually end now with snow and sub-zero temperatures. The climbing itself becomes more of a challenge. Unlike much of the hike to Everest Base Camp, which is characterised by well-trodden paths filled with droves of trekkers, we have strayed 'off piste'. Our diversion takes us up towards this lonely wind-blown pass, scrambling over unmarked fields of glacial moraine and scree on all fours. We don't see another soul for most of the day. Perhaps the endeavour is ill-advised given our woeful equipment, but it is also exhilarating. Happily, we do at last come across a proper guide attempting the same pass, albeit on his own and tag onto him. The Cho La is surely our hardest challenge and greatest achievement to date. Certainly the most exhausting.

Some of the other tourists we have met in the lodges on the way up suffer from altitude sickness. Others are old hands. We meet one group of Australians – the 'Adeladies' as they call themselves – one of whom describes herself as 'tough as old boots'. Who are we to deny it? It's her ninth trip to Nepal. In another lodge we get to know an American called Chad Kellogg, who has summited Everest four times. We are shocked when he tells us his wife died in a climbing accident only three months before. He watched her drop from a rope below him and plummet to her death, he tells us, quite matter of factly. Some of the trekkers are rank amateurs like ourselves. Others, like Chad, have the obsessive glint in their eye. It doesn't take long to mark people out as one or the other.

Meanwhile, our own particular complaint, besides the altitude headaches and nausea that most suffer, is the cheapness of our gear. As always, you get what you pay for, and when it comes to our gear, we haven't paid very much. Thus, the nights are undeniably chilly and uncomfortable. The lodge at Lobuche is a particular low point. The place is filthy and freezing cold, equipped with yak-dung fire burners which prove entirely inadequate to the task. The room is only big enough for one person to change at a time. This is all especially disheartening after tackling the Cho La Pass which has left us shattered from over seven hours of hard walking. Fortunately our final abode at serious altitude, in a place called Gorak Shep at 5,140m, is a good deal more amenable, passing even Hicky's more exacting standards.

It's from here that we launch our attack on Everest Base Camp, which is to be the upper limit of our climb. In the event, we get within sight of it, but it looks like such a miserable little enclave of tents and climbing paraphernalia, huddled in the shadow of a huge cliff face which blots out any view of Everest, that we don't bother climbing all the way down to it. Instead we decide to climb a peak overlooking the Base Camp called Kala Pattar, recommended to us by a Swedish hiker, who tells us its summit sits at 5,900m.

We slog our way up there and it is worth every bead of sweat. Everest is visible from the top. So close it looks *huge*, a great looming presence at once awesome and intimidating. Even as we are watching, we see a massive avalanche break away and tumble down the far side of the valley. From that peak, we can gaze down on the multi-coloured tents of Base Camp and pity the fools who have committed themselves to tackling such a monster.

'Feel like a crack at it?' I ask Hicky.

'No thanks, mate. This is quite far enough for me.' I have to agree with him. In this flimsy pair of trousers, with zips down the sides that are broken and flashing exposed thighs, there's winging it, and then there's taking the piss.

With our own personal goal now achieved, there are many smiles, high fives and general rejoicing that we can now turn our toes downhill and commence the homeward leg. This we do after a celebratory slap-up breakfast of fried eggs on toast (a rare luxury) back in Gorak Shep, already five hundred metres below our summit.

We then practically run all the way back to Namche

Bazar in under two days. It's taken us nine to climb from there up to Kala Pattar. Of course, the ever-thickening oxygen helps. We feel like supermen. I don't believe I've ever felt so physically strong – a wonderful feeling when only a few days before even leaving one's bed to take a leak in an outdoor latrine would leave me breathless.

In Namche Bazar we go some way to assuaging our ravening hunger. And this time we make absolutely sure that we stay in a more hospitable lodge. We awake then for the final day feeling refreshed, refuelled and in fine fettle. The last climb of the whole trek, however, is hell. 'It went on and on and on and on,' I record in my journal. 'And neither Hicky nor I had any motivation to deal with it or each other.'

Hicky

Once we have managed at last to haul our carcasses over the final summit, Lukla appears below us like Shangri-La to our weary limbs. We take full advantage of its amenities – showering, eating and drinking in that order. Indeed, our return becomes something of a celebration as more and more fellow trekkers join our merry company. We are reunited with a young gap-year Brit with a troop of sherpas (not all in his pay) and another American couple who have just completed the same journey as us. One of the sherpas suggests retiring to a nearby watering hole he knows – a veritable nest of sherpas – where we could partake of a local brew called Chang. This, a rather potent drop of rice beer. Here we enjoy probably our most authentic taste of Nepalese culture, squeezed onto benches in a small dark room with only a gang of rascally sherpas as drinking buddies, knocking back this milky white liquid from battered tin mugs. There's an open fire in the corner over which our hosts fry chopped potatoes swimming in chilli and some equally delicious (if a little tough) cubes of yak meat.

All this proves a fine antidote to the aches and pains (both physical and mental) suffered over the last two weeks.

Back in Kathmandu, we kick our heels for a few days, by turns recovering, taking excessively long baths, eating prodigious quantities of all kinds of food – Asian or Western it didn't matter – seeing that Netty got a good servicing, sightseeing, arguing (which always happens when we are in one place for too long), and generally girding up our loins in readiness for the launch into the next big leg of our journey: the highlands of Tibet (otherwise known as the Friendship Highway).

We are still waiting here for our visa green light into China on April 13th (2010), the day that marks six months exactly since our grand departure. We make a plan to go out that evening and celebrate in a swanky restaurant, maybe drink a half-decent bottle of red wine, but as the afternoon progresses it starts pouring with rain outside. My limbs are feeling particularly inert.

'Let's not bother,' I tell Tom.

'What do you mean, not bother? I'm looking forward to this.'

'It's pissing it down. I never like going out when it's raining.'

'If that's the case, you live in the wrong bloody country,' he says – rather huffily I think.

With the mood somewhat soured, our semi-anniversary feast is pulled in favour of something more functional (and a lot nearer to the hotel). The following day, there's no doubt at all that I have fallen out of favour with Tom.

All is made well, however, when he insists on our having the dinner anyway, two nights later, where he very kindly presents me with a Kukri knife as an early birthday gift, together with a badge commemorating our epic trek. The badge reads, 'Cho La Pass 2010: To hell and back.'

'To heaven and back sounds more appropriate,' I suggest.

'Mmm,' he agrees. Then adds, 'Slightly less gnarly though.'

The time to move on has now arrived. The Great Dragon calls. So off we must fly into the Middle Kingdom.

NINE

Crossing the Land of the Dragon –
Kathmandu to Kunming

Tom

Our final stop on the way out of Nepal before we cross into China is by way of a place called the Last Resort – appropriately enough – where we feel it would be churlish to pass up the chance to attend a Nepalese music festival. The Fifth Sundance Festival proves a very definite hit – especially given expectations could hardly have been lower – that is until the heavens open in rather spectacular fashion, putting quite a dampener on the second half of the evening. Fortuitously, this not only renders the music festival a wash-out but also somewhat cools the ardour of Hickman, who has entangled himself in a romantic clinch with a Welsh rugby player. She plays prop forward; naturally, a fact which I may have to bring up several hundred times in conversation over the days that follow.

Sporting not insubstantial hangovers, we are nevertheless on parade at the appointed hour the following morning to mount up in the Netster in readiness to endure the horrendous single-lane dirt track which will get us to the Chinese border. The road climbs up and up, eventually leading us to a bridge which spans an apparently bottomless chasm.

'Very James Bond,' observes Hicky. By now, you will have realised that there is barely a situation or landscape which Hickman cannot relate to some movie or other which he has seen.

'I assume you mean *Goldeneye*.'

'What else!'

It's not an entirely inappropriate reference given that we are required to wait on the Nepalese side of the bridge while our government-appointed Chinese guide walks across the bridge to meet us. I should explain. When it comes to overlanding, the bureaucratic burden is inevitably heaviest in China and especially Tibet. In order to obtain our entry visa with Netty, we have had to file a detailed itinerary with the tourism board who have approved it, subject to our taking on board a Communist-Party-accredited guide for the entire span of our drive through China. Thus, her long walk across the bridge has something of the feel of a Cold War prisoner exchange. This feeling is only further compounded when we discover that the road we are about to follow is called the Road of a Thousand Souls because so many labourers died in its making.

As to be expected, at first the Chinese side of the border seems alien, confusing and just a little bit terrifying. The uniforms are starchier, the buttons more polished, the expressions sterner. The presence of our guide, who introduces herself as Penny, certainly softens what would otherwise be a very hard landing. Our first impressions of her are: 'very nice, with a warm smile and most importantly, very organised'. (Thus reads my journal.) This last is of prime importance given the vast amounts of paperwork to be overcome. For this reason alone, the leg of the journey that we are about to embark upon is not to be undertaken lightly.

One of the first oddities to contend with is the new time zone. Officially, the whole of China is on Beijing's time zone so the 'evenings' come unnaturally early in the cycle of the day. Simply by crossing the border bridge we lost four hours of our day.

From the border, the road heads ever upwards. We fill up with -20 degrees diesel at the first gas station we come to, in preparation for the days ahead.

As we head higher into these remarkable mountains we find ourselves driving across a dusty orange plateau, surrounded on all sides by the monstrous Himalayas. We pull over to take photos and soak in the view.

From nowhere a pair of men seem to spring up from the side of the road. Where they appear from or what they are doing there, we never discover, given that there is nothing visible for 360 degrees on the plateau. They seem to be lamas (Tibetan monks), albeit extremely rustic ones. We stop and exchange greetings. They smile toothlessly at us and then scatter grain in front of the wheels of the car. We understand this to be some kind of blessing for our onward journey. The encounter feels almost mystical given the extraordinary surroundings.

Our first stopover in Tibet is the border town of Nielamu which sits at 3,700m above sea level, but after our trekking, our bodies seem to have acclimatised to the altitude (at least for the moment). I fall asleep that night still trying to come to terms with the fact that we are driving an English Land Rover through the mythical land of Tibet, the images of its mountain slopes covered in newly budding rhododendron bushes flashing across heavy eyelids.

Hicky

The Chinese seem to take a far more pragmatic approach to reaching the top of the world. Forget trekking. On the Tibetan side, you can drive all the way to Everest Base Camp, which is our next port of call. Having said that, the drive is a bone-rattling, arse-numbing experience, barely seeing the speedometer needle rise above the 20mph mark once in the long hours it takes to drive all the way up to 5,300m. But the scenery is extraordinary. Naked hills and mountainsides, bleak in appearance, ochre red in colour or just a dull brown, totally devoid of any visible vegetation and of course with no trees at all (we are well above the treeline). The road snakes past rock formations that defy any kind of description, writhing left and right in dozens and dozens of switchbacks, while the surface deteriorates to grit and rubble. The fact that the landscape is so open and the air so sharp means you can see the road stretch out for miles and miles ahead of you, which is not a little disheartening when your progress is reduced to a crawl.

But then you eventually crest the last climb and there she is before you in all her glory. Mount Everest – *Chomolungma* in the Tibetan tongue – visible from summit to base, the wind blasting a huge sheet of snow off its eastern face, which looks like hair streaming in its wake. It is an astonishing sight.

After four hours of driving, Penny gives us the option to continue on to Base Camp for another hour or find a local guest house in the last village heading up there. We opt for the latter and are very happy to be treated to our first taste of authentic Tibetan hospitality. We spend the evening chatting about our first impressions of the Tibetans. We both agree they seem extremely friendly and interested in us. (Perhaps that's not surprising given how difficult it is to get up here.) Their faces are very striking, their skin weather-beaten to a degree you could hardly believe possible, and their clothing very distinctive. The women wear some sort of traditional striped apron fastened by an enormous silver-buckled belt, while the men we have seen nearly all wear a kind of red woollen turban coiled around their heads to support their long black plaited hair. They also have bone rings woven into their plaits and distinctive blue earrings. Their footwear consists of bands of colourful cloth wrapped round and round their feet and calves against the cold. Everything is colourful up here. Their clothes, their houses, their prayer flags adorning the many high places, and even their ponies and yaks are decorated with multi-coloured tack, red tassels and even woollen earrings.

'I think I'd want everything I owned to be as cheery as possible if I lived in a landscape this bleak,' Tom concludes.

We are served sweet tea which becomes an instant favourite. Perhaps a little less appetising is the sight that greets us when we are shown the kitchen. Hanging from the wall are objects resembling old wasp nests which we soon learn from Penny are in fact sheep fat wrapped in sheep's intestine. Beside these is a leg of lamb with hoof and fur still intact. The outside larder has no fewer than five sheep carcasses hanging from the wall. The ambient temperature is so low at that altitude that there is no need to smoke or salt the meat to preserve it.

'Not sure what you're supposed to do up here if you

don't like sheep,' I wonder aloud.

That evening we sit pouring endless sweet tea down our throats in the village '*can-ting*' (a.k.a. canteen). There's a table seating a handful of policemen (all ethnically Han Chinese) playing mah-jong across the room from another, around which are gathered a few local shepherds. It is hard to know which group throws more surreptitious looks at the other. We suspect this may be a glimpse of the rather tense relations between the native Tibetans and their Chinese overlords in this part of the world.

The next day we cover the last hour of driving up to Everest Base Camp on the Tibetan side – having expended considerably less energy than we did on the Nepalese side. (About which we feel not a shred of guilt whatsoever.) The Chinese have a rather infuriating system whereby you can drive to within about three kilometres of the official Base Camp. But then you have to park up and take a bus the rest of the way. As Penny explains, 'This to protect the Mount Everest.' Baffled, we park the car and head to the bus stop.

Before we jump on the bus, we notice the 'hotel' we were supposed to have stayed in the night before. It is nothing more than a single-room tent which, given the mercury hit around minus ten degrees, we are pleased we avoided. Our hubris at being able to drive (most of the way) to Base Camp instead of trekking it means we are woefully underdressed. Feet, hands, legs, everything is freezing cold. To make matters worse, after the bus, we walk up towards the knoll from which we will be able to see Mount Everest in all its glory, only to be thwarted within fifty metres of the crest at a checkpoint where, we are assured, we definitely do *not* have the requisite permit to summit the knoll. (Alas, it languishes, forgotten, in the car.) This does not do wonders for our mood, and only stirs our ire against the pointless obstinacy of the guard. But perhaps it is also an interesting, if maddening, insight into Chinese officialdom.

On this occasion, we concede the field and retire without our show-stopper view of Everest, and we are soon back on our bone-cruncher of a road, trundling lazily back downhill the way we came.

Tom

'Theirs is an extremely harsh life but one that they seem to embrace with open arms.' This is my journal comment after passing a group of Tibetan farmers scratching out some sort of subsistence from earth that looks about as barren as the Sahara. A naive assessment on reflection, but in my defence, it is probably borne out of the fact that everyone we pass has time to spare us a broad smile.

The drive to Shigatse (or Xigaze) – Tibet's second largest city after Lhasa – is equally epic, and the road surface, once we are back on the main highway, is good. In Shigatse, our guide Penny reminds us that we are going to take our Chinese driving test here. After installing ourselves in our hotel – in which hot showers, a proper loo and a half-decent bed cause much excitement – we take ourselves off to the police station where I take two Han Chinese officers for a spin in the Netster. Both she and I appear to pass with flying colours. After a lot of hanging around, we then have to endure an interminable lecture (with Penny translating) from one of the officers about Chinese speed limits, the value of human life etc., etc. – which, given what we will soon discover about the general quality of Chinese driving, is a bit rich. At this point, we imagine we are free to go but, oh no! There is a physical test as well – height, weight, temperature, blood pressure and an eye test. We suspect this bureaucratic quagmire might engulf us for the rest of the day, but we are saved at last, thanks to some sterling desk-jumping from our stalwart, if diminutive, guide. We leave with two brand new Chinese driving licences and some temporary Chinese number plates with which to adorn Netty's front and back.

All of this means that of sightseeing on our first day in Shigatse, we do precious little; despite that, the place does seem quite remarkable. The monastery dominates the town, perched in dramatic fashion on an outcrop of rock like a medieval citadel, splendid against the clear skies with its sheer white walls and red slate roofing.

Hitherto the food has been a pleasant surprise for us. We discover that it bears no resemblance whatsoever to so-called Chinese food in England and we are enjoying becoming more accomplished with chopsticks. Opinion, however, is divided during our evening in Shigatse. We ask Penny to choose us something characteristically Chinese and unusual. She comes up with preserved duck eggs, known as 'pídàn' or 'Thousand-Year-Eggs'. These are pale blue duck eggs packed in clay and left to 'age'. The result, once boiled, is extraordinary. Basically a boiled rotten egg, where the white has turned translucent brown, and the yolk is a bluish/purple colour. Chopped up and served with various herbs and spices they are utterly delicious.

The next day we wander around Tashi Lhunpo, Shigatse's six-hundred-year-old monastery, second only to Lhasa in terms of importance (and holiness), according to the Gelug school of Tibetan Buddhism, and the traditional seat of successive Panchen Lamas. (The Panchen Lama ranks just below the Dalai Lama, 'Panchen' being

an abbreviation of two words meaning 'Great Scholar'.)
The monastery's full name, on the other hand, means 'all
fortune and glory gathered here' or 'heap of glory,' which
given its precarious position on top of a sheer rocky hill
seems appropriate. One British officer of the East India
Company, who visited the monastery in the late 18th
century, described it in terms far more eloquent than
anything I could produce:

> If the magnificence of the place was to be increased
> by any external cause, none could more superbly
> have adorned its numerous gilded canopies and
> turrets than the sun rising in full splendour directly
> opposite. It presented a view wonderfully beautiful
> and brilliant; the effect was little short of magic, and
> it made an impression which no time will ever efface
> from my mind.

We are treated to something similar. Its partial destruc-
tion is, perhaps, no less interesting than its beautiful
construction. Two-thirds of the monastery's buildings
were destroyed during the Chinese Cultural Revolution. Fortunately these were mostly the residences of
the four thousand monks living there at the time, while
the monastery itself was not as extensively damaged as
many other religious structures in Tibet during that
time (mainly because it was already in Chinese-held
territory). However, in 1966, Red Guards led a mob into
the monastery to smash up statues, burn scriptures and
open the stupas containing the relics of the 5th to the
9th Panchen Lamas, and threw their bones and decaying
bodies into the river. Some of the remains were saved by
locals and in 1985 the 10th Panchen Lama had a new stupa

built to house them. It was finished and consecrated in 1989, just six days before he himself died and was therein laid to rest.

There's another monastery to view in the next town, Jingzi, notable for its frescos as well as its towering stupas topped with gold and surrounded by a high stone wall, which makes the place seem quite fabulous (in its literal sense). In every direction you care to glance there are prayer flags fluttering in the wind.

When we enter the main hall it is exactly as you might imagine the inside of a Buddhist monastery to be. Incense burns and the light is dim and mysterious. In between the broad red pillars, prayer-cushions are laid out on the floor with each monk's cloak propped up in their own imitation-sitting position marking their spot. Beside each cushion lies the traditional mohican-styled hat the monks wear. Its atmosphere and solemnity create a deep impression on both of us.

At lunchtime, I cheer Hicky up – it's his birthday after all – by buying him his first beer since entering Tibet (which we reckon is pretty good going given our track record).

I should say a word on Penny. Our indefatigable guide is certainly proving her worth in terms of bureaucracy and meal selection. (This last would be a total minefield – or lottery, depending on your viewpoint – were it not for her discerning eye and ability to read the menus.) We are beginning to form the impression, however, that the information which she is willing to impart about the various places we visit is all, rather dismally, going to toe the strictest and straightest of Communist Party lines. We realise that she must be on a pretty short leash. When in full flow, she sounds like a propaganda messaging service, whether we ask her about the places we're seeing or more general questions about China. She is never without her clipboard. And on the road, she is seated in the back, separated from us by Netty's cockpit cage – the 'dog cage' as Hicky calls it – rather pitifully clinging onto the grill as she intones the many achievements of Chairman Mao. One of her favourite soundbites is that, 'Chairman Mao only make three mistake his whole life.' Only one of these can I recall: that Mao smothered the Chinese people with *too* much love. Hicky's response at the time: 'Yes, smothered them with so much "love" that several million of them starved to death.'

The lessons in propaganda aside, we do come to form a grudging respect for her, in time. She will show herself pretty hardy between here and the Laos border, putting up with the raw conditions, the long hours on the road, and some very far from salubrious hostelries along the way without even a whisper of complaint. For all that, Hicky still can't resist nicknaming her Penny Pig behind her back.

'She smells like sour milk,' he says in an attempt to justify himself.

Hicky
The next port of call is the most holy lake in Tibet: Yamzho Yumco. We have to struggle through the ever-more-frequent roadblocks to get there – perhaps a sign of the political stranglehold which Beijing has on the capital of Tibet.

The lake is another extraordinary sight to add to the sensory feast we have been treated to on our journey across the roof of the world – everywhere steep-sided bronze-coloured hills, just dirt, no trees, which tumble down into the most brilliant turquoise lake I have ever seen. Somewhere these pristine waters empty into the long Brahmaputra River which flows many thousands of miles back into India through the province of Arunachal Pradesh and onwards, by then filled with all kinds of filth and pollution.

It is April 23rd – my birthday. I couldn't have picked a place that feels further away from home in which to spend it.

Before we reach Lhasa we stop off at the site of one of the British Empire's less edifying moments. In December 1903 an expedition set out from British India, led by Lieutenant Colonel Younghusband, to march on Lhasa, ostensibly to resolve a border dispute between the Tibetans and the Indians of the province of Sikkim to the south, but it was also part of the larger Great Game playing out between the Russians and the British across Central Asia at that time. The Tibetans resisted the British advance to Lhasa, but armed with antiquated muskets, the Tibetan troops were no match for the British Maxim machine guns. They were slaughtered. That didn't stop the Governor-General of India issuing a campaign medal.

Following in these rather ignominious footsteps, we probably deserve the entanglement we get ourselves in upon arrival in Lhasa. The by-now familiar motif of arriving in a big Asian city and becoming hopelessly lost is reprised in some style this time round. This is made considerably worse by Penny Pig (or PP as we shall call her) whose refusal to read a map in order to locate our hotel only compounds the difficulty she has in making herself understood to the local Tibetans. Whether through wilful obstinacy or pure ignorance, very few Lhasans speak any kind of Mandarin. Tom appears ready to throttle her after her stubborn refusal to read the map rather than continue in her futile attempts to navigate by the road signs. We must have found our hotel eventually, but I'll be damned if I can remember how.

Lhasa is squarely on the tourist trail and the city is full of foreigners, most of whom have arrived in buses from the east. Mingling with them and the droves of domestic tourists, we dutifully trawl around the famous sites. The Jokhang Temple, the holiest site in Tibet, and of course the iconic Potala Palace, piled up against the hillside in all its splendour. Our enjoyment and interest in these are tempered by the relentless propaganda spilling from PP's lips as we wander around. One example that borders on the absurd: in the Potala Palace, she shows us two enormous statues made of gold. The sign tells us they weigh four tonnes. Penny insists they are nine tonnes. Challenging her on this, showing her the plaque, she would accept nothing less than her 'official' figure.

She makes much of China's liberation of Tibet, although from whom exactly China is supposed to have liberated Tibet is a question she is unable to answer. Of particular irony to us is the location of the Freedom of Tibet monument, a giant concrete monstrosity, which sits directly across the square from the former seat of the exiled Dalai Lama. Two armed soldiers stand guard in full military regalia, to our mind rubbing salt in an open wound.

In the afternoon, it is pleasant to amble around the Dalai Lama's Summer Palace where it is nice simply to see some greenery after the hundreds of miles of dirt and rocks that we have just crossed.

My belly is in some trouble. Possibly this has something to do with our last lunch on the road to Lhasa. 'Hicky-

A sprinkling of corn – spiritual blessings on the friendship highway. Near Tingri, Tibet.

Tom and Netty admiring one of the stunningly blue high lakes we passed in Tibet. Nagaze County, Tibet.

Below: the expedition in front of Everest Base Camp, Tibet.

Until we meet again – with our indefatigable guide Penny Chen at the Chinese–Laos border. Boten border crossing.

The dwarf village – with the King and his entourage. South of Kunming, China.

Rice paddies – even the amateur photographer nails this shot. Yuanyang rice terraces, Yunnan Province.

Camping American-style – back in the west and back in the roof tent. Yosemite National Park.

Tom soaking up the view, happily perched on the edge of a 2,000-foot vertical drop. Grand Canyon South Rim, Arizona.

Winged It – the last night. Mission accomplished. Tannersville
Cranberry Bog, Pennsylvania.

Tom,' (her collective noun for us) 'you want pork berry?'
We gave her an enthusiastic affirmative to this question,
and sat relishing the prospect of something akin to
a plate of good old English pork belly for lunch. Alas,
when the dish arrived, her 'pork belly' proved to be the
rubbery, white stomach lining, not the delicious layers of
slow cooked meat, fat and crackling we had hoped for.
It tasted as revolting as it sounds and, I believe, gave me
food poisoning to boot. If that wasn't enough to clean
me out, the Chinese 'hot pot' – a kind of meat fondue
suffused with very strong chilli sauce – which we try one
evening in Lhasa finishes the job. I am a hollow reed by
this point.

It's probably a good thing then that we are delayed in
Lhasa for another day when PP is unable to secure the
necessary permits to continue on our journey – which
sends her into panic mode but gives me some time to
recover before we set out on the weary road from Lhasa
down to Chengdu.

East of Lhasa we continue to follow the route G318
which deteriorates in quality quite drastically as soon as
we leave the city. Landslides are a common occurrence. It
is very slow going, although the scenery continues to be
as dramatic as before. The road often follows the contours
of a vast mountainside, falling away steeply below us
on one side. It is narrow, too. For two vehicles to pass
often requires the car on the uphill side of the road to
rev straight up the scree at a steep angle in order to allow
the outer vehicle to squeeze by, before carefully releasing
the brake and dropping back down onto the road. With
the giddy drop-off on one side, this makes for some hairy
moments, although both of us become quite adept at the
manoeuvre.

The distances we are covering are fairly big but so too are the hours at the wheel. The first day after Lhasa we drive for eight full hours in order to do 265 miles. Even when the going is better, the police at each roadblock control one's speed by checking the time elapsed since one passed the last checkpoint. To avoid paying a fine, one must not arrive before the appointed hour.

For all the road's frustrations, the scenery is stunning. This is driving in its purest form. Long hours, huge distances, music blaring, not a lot of conversation, and little of any note to record about the towns and villages we pass through. But when we descend below the treeline for the first time since Nepal, the green of the highland forests is of an intensity we have seldom, if ever, experienced. It's late April so spring is about to burst out across the land. The road follows a river brim-full with glacial meltwaters, blue as the sky above our heads. When it widens into a lake we pull over, just short of the little town of Ranwu. Tom promptly declares it the most beautiful lake he's ever seen. To mark the moment, we pull out our deckchairs and sit by the water's edge as the sun slowly falls behind the surrounding peaks. I have a go at painting the scene whilst Tom sits sunning himself and drinking a beer. It is entirely serene.

Tom
We are starting to realise that towns are PP's Achilles heel. She gets in a flap every time we reach our day's destination while she tries to figure out the location of the next nondescript hotel she has booked us into. In one place, she resorts to hiring a local taxi for us to follow to the hotel, which somehow results in our getting pulled over by the police. Fortunately her ability to obtain all the

necessary permits is pretty much faultless, so we always have the correct paperwork whenever challenged by the local constabulary.

From Ranwu, she warns us that the next day will be a long one. We are heading back up into the high ground again, with one or two high altitude passes to traverse. We are ready for the challenge. But we manage to make the day considerably harder than it needs to be when we stop for petrol at the foot of one particularly laborious climb. Reaching the top, some two and a half hours later, we pull over to admire the view – which is jaw-dropping – of the road which we have just followed on its wending way up the mountain. A fellow motorist, also pulled over for a break, comes over to admire Netty. After a few seconds, he starts trying to tell me something and pointing at the fuel cap. Or rather, where the fuel cap *should* be... Nearly five hours later we are back in the same spot, having had to return to the petrol station where a rather sheepish pump attendant hands us the cap he forgot to put back on.

Thus, when we finally pull into the little town of Zogang that evening after more than ten brutal hours on the road, we are exhausted. We have achieved only a hundred kilometres all day. Again, we are installed in a very forgettable hotel, albeit one crammed with several busloads of Chinese tourists on their way up to Lhasa. Hicky is first in the shower and first down to dinner. In his haste to wet his lips with a local beer and fill his recovering belly, he later tells me, he ran down the stairs and into the bar where a group of ten Chinese women sipping mai tais pointed at him and burst out laughing. Shocked and on the back foot, he bolted into the next room which happened to be the dining room – something on the scale of a large ballroom – to find every table filled with Chinese. At his entry, the entire room stopped talking, chopsticks half-raised to lips, and turned to stare at him for a solid five seconds, before they collapsed into gales of laughter. With his sore backside and tender stomach, being laughed at by two throngs of various Chinese was more than poor Hickman could endure, beating a hasty retreat back to the room in search of reinforcements.

All the way along the road from Lhasa to Kangding we pass pilgrims on their way to this most holy city. Knowing what lay ahead for them, one had nothing but admiration as they dragged handcarts uphill. We saw many of them performing a prostration by the roadside, and presumably most of them didn't indulge in the luxury of staying in hotels like the tourists who come by bus. But, without a doubt, they deserve it.

It's another two days of 'pure driving' – as we call it – to reach the larger regional hub of Kangding. Twelve-hour days, covering a mere hundred miles on the first of those, often on single carriageways, negotiating landslides using our newly acquired passing skills, and spending more time than we care for sitting in gridlock behind the numerous lorries that ply route G318 as we and our fellow road users attempt to work out a way of navigating nature's latest obstacle. This bitter pill was sweetened by the scenery of course, at all times. I record one scene that particularly strikes me in my journal:

It was a particularly pretty village, spread out and not [merely] lining the roadside. The houses were all painted in their usual bright colours and the villagers were outside in the sun looking very relaxed. Behind the village were some small and tidy fields all dotted with trees covered in a fantastic pink blossom while two or three yak-powered ploughs tilled the soil around their trunks.

In Kangding, we meet up with my old friend, Arthur Burnand, who had endured twelve separate bus routes to get himself up here all the way from Shanghai. This is not as bad for him as it might sound since he has been living in China for five years (he went straight out after university) and speaks Mandarin fluently. Nevertheless, it is a testament to our friendship that he is prepared to make the effort to join us.

Kangding is not like any of the towns we have yet passed through in China. It is a bustling infrastructure hub, filled with businesses and restaurants and bars – a foretaste of many of the other cities we will pass through on our way out of China. We have left Tibet proper behind us now and crossed into the province of Sichuan, famed for its spicy foods and frontier-land energy. Arthur's ability to speak Mandarin makes navigating menus considerably easier and we give PP the night off. We spend the evening catching up, drinking *baijiu* (pronounced 'bai-jo') – a truly potent drink Arthur introduces us to which reminds us of Japanese sake but tastes considerably worse. Hicky leaves us to it after a while and we continue drinking and chatting late into the night.

It's probably this which causes our most serious incident on the road the following day on the drive from Kangding down to the comparative lowlands of Chengdu. I am driving, mainly out of hubris, declaring myself fit as a fiddle, but in reality probably still under the influence of the infamous (and evil) *baijiu*.

We squeeze the three of us in the front seat, with PP

in the back on the other side of the dog cage. We are driving along behind a bus when one of its passengers pulls down the window and throws an empty plastic bottle into the undergrowth. At that moment we happen to be passing through a particularly attractive part of the countryside, everything in full bloom with the arrival of spring and the three of us become a sweltering ball of righteous indignation – that this philistine should have the gall to pollute his beautiful environment with such callous indifference.

'The problem is a lack of education,' says Arthur. 'Let's teach him a lesson.'

'What do you have in mind?' I ask.

'I know,' he continues. 'Seeing as he chucked a bottle out of the window, let's throw one back in. Sort of like nature biting back!'

'Excellent idea,' agrees Hicky, passing over a suitable projectile and with that the matter is settled.

Netty being a right-hand drive car, and with China being a right-hand-lane country, it fell to me as driver to also be the administrator of our rapidly formulated brand of environmental justice. I accelerate, bottle in hand and window wound down, to overtake the bus.

'Ready,' cries Arthur. 'Here it comes!'

Hungover and determined not to miss my mark, I concentrate intently on the target about a third of the way up the bus's flank. The window draws level and with my eye firmly on the prize I launch the bottle cleanly through the miscreant's window.

Any sense of satisfaction is extremely short lived. The human body will naturally go where the eyes are looking and this was no exception. Like something straight out of a Hollywood car chase the Netster rams the bus before ripping its bull bar all the way down one side.

The next instant, the bus is careering off the road into an area of grit and gravel and the last any of us see is it fishtailing violently from left to right as it disappears into an enormous cloud of dust. While this drama has unfolded in front of us, I have brought Netty to a halt. As the dust begins to settle we see to our enormous relief that the bus is still upright. There is a long pause, one that I will remember for the rest of my life. I look to my left and see two dumbstruck faces staring back at me, knowing that the look on my face is no different. The options are flying through my mind, no one is talking, so I rapidly come to a decision. With a muttered, 'F**k that,' I ram the Netster back into gear and speed off down the road. In all likelihood, apart from a hell of a fright, none of the passengers are any the worse for wear and I am not about to wait around to provide explanations of our behaviour to the Chinese police. However fluent Arthur may be, I don't believe he would have found the words to talk us out of that one.

The drama is not quite over, however. PP is going completely bananas in the back. She was dozing when it happened, so now she is screaming to know what is going on.

'Nothing, nothing at all,' sings Hicky soothingly. (Fortunately the visibility from Netty's rear seat, with no rear windows and the dog cage, is such that one cannot see very much of anything from back there.)

Met with a wall of silence she is just starting to calm down as we approach the next village and goes back to looking at her phone. I am not calm at all and my paranoia is validated as I notice a very fraught-looking man on a mobile telephone standing beside the road about a hundred metres ahead. Seeing the rather distinctive Netty from afar he immediately becomes extremely animated and jumps into the middle of the road, waving both arms in the air and gesticulating wildly for us to stop.

Silence in the cab. Another muttered 'F**k that,' and I take Netty up onto the pavement, round the man and bump back down on the other side.

Penny, bounced off her little bench in the back as we hit the curb and deposited on the floor, immediately goes ballistic again. Hicky and Arthur placate her with some talk of speed bumps while I sit in somewhat terrified silence wondering whether I am making good my escape or simply digging a deeper hole for myself.

Penny's suspicions are further aroused when we tell her we no longer want to go to the only local tourist attraction that we had been due to stop at en route to Chengdu. 'Something happen back there! You tell me what happen. Why you no wanna go no more?' We stonewall her, claiming tiredness.

We brook no further delay in getting to Chengdu, pressing on in shocked silence, while fully expecting police sirens at every single moment. Upon arrival we make straight for a high-end hotel, hoping for a likely place with an underground car park. Totally undeservedly, Providence seems to be smiling on us and we find such a place. We manage to get PP out and away from the car without her noticing the huge smear of blue paint down the entire length of one side of the car. We don't return to the car for three days, quite deliberately. Netty has now become a crime scene.

Hicky

Chengdu is wreathed in a cloud of alcohol. (More of it.) As a city, it has a great vibe to it, modern, forward-looking, but kind of gritty as well. It reminds me of New York. Arthur immediately plugs us into the expat life for the two days we are there. We experience our first proper Chinese nightlife, patronising nightclubs in the guise of two famous western rock stars (Tom and I) accompanied by their interpreter (Arthur). Perhaps Arthur's ability to speak Mandarin is the only convincing thing about this pretence, but that is enough to get us special treatment and the attention of some members of the fairer clientele in the place. PP, meanwhile, takes a couple of well-earned days off. (Chengdu is her hometown.)

One morning, with Tom nursing a particularly nasty little hangover, I bet him that he can't down a shot of whisky and a Long Island Iced Tea left standing from the night before. Tom counters that if he does, then I am to buy him dinner in the Mandarin Oriental in Bangkok. The stakes agreed, he manfully sees it away...

'Oh well,' I sportingly sigh. 'At least we now have something to look forward to in Bangkok.'

When we bid our farewells to Arthur and make ready to move on in our progress towards southern China, we are already looking ahead to Laos and Thailand where we are going to spend some time with Tom's brother, Charlie, and his girlfriend, Mima. Perhaps it is for this reason that the next section of our journey doesn't seem to loom very large in the context of the whole experience. But also, after the intensity of the Tibetan plateau, how can the provinces of Chongqing, Guizhou or even Sichuan measure up?

Yes, we see pandas in Chengdu and, moving on to

Chongqing, we visit the Three Gorges on the Yangtze River, both of which are impressive enough. But we are covering big distances, pushing on for the south. It is really only when we reach the province of Yunnan that we are struck once again by our surroundings. The land of perpetual spring, Yunnan is truly lovely. The terraced paddy fields, the rolling hills, the tree blossom filling the air with its scent.

But before we come to all that, we decide we have had enough of PP's itinerary and take matters into our own hands. Bored at home and researching his brother's current location, Charlie has emailed Tom about a place called the Dwarf Kingdom. This is not some hidden valley in the vein of Shangri-La (the mythical – and fictional – land supposed to exist somewhere in this neck of the woods). No. It is in fact a theme park, of sorts – entirely peopled by little people. It is situated just south of the city of Kunming – the provincial capital of Yunnan. Its official name is Xiao Airen WangGuo – which translates as the Kingdom of the Little People. Supposedly it is a community of people with dwarfism who have created entertainments for the amusement and interest of paying customers. But the community itself has its own services and facilities, all operated by little people. For visitors, the place features comic performances, or they dress up as various characters in history such as Genghis Khan and Marco Polo, to name two you might have heard of. Our overlanding expedition, however, is not your average visitor, and upon entry we are escorted straight to the mushroom-shaped mini-palace for an audience with the King and his fairy Queen, where our every move is watched by the dwarf secret service.

Of course, the whole concept has its detractors, the

Chinese answer to which is that it gives employment opportunities to people who otherwise might struggle to find work. We are not sure where we stand on the question, but it seems a better use of our money than the two hundred yuan PP would have had us pay to visit China's largest waterfall.

The rice terraces around the town of Yuanyang are, perhaps, less controversial, and incredibly striking to view for the first time. They seem to fall in a slippery cascade off the hillside, the bright blue skies and scudding white clouds reflected in the surface of the water filling each paddy-field. And gazing around each valley, the stepped appearance of each sequence of terraces gives the impression of some sort of monumental staircase, leading up and up to a giant's palace in the sky.

We are somewhat staggered to learn that every single plant one can see in the landscape is planted, tended and harvested by hand. Happily, this is one landscape where our photos seem to do it justice. The climate has changed. Gone are the mountains and the freezing nights. We can feel the hot humidity of south-east Asia beckoning us closer each day.

By now we are closing in on the tail end of China. But each new town seems to inspire new heights of incompetence and confusion from our inimitable guide, Ms PP. Every town we come to, we can expect to get lost for a good half an hour before getting our bearings. Sad to admit, after such an epic journey, I am looking forward to parting company with her. But I'm more worried whether Tom is going to make it to the border without doing her a serious injury. I am afraid that we have not managed to penetrate more than the one-dimension she has been willing to show to us over the few thousand miles we have covered together. Friendship has not blossomed. A harmonious union has not taken root. Alas. But one still cannot fail to admire her intrepidity, to be willing to travel from one extreme border of China to another with a pair of reprobate westerners for company. For this reason alone, we send her off, if not with our fondest love and blessing, at least with a decent tip.

In Mengla, the last town before the Laos border, we repack Netty and give her a good clean, making sure that no foreign articles have crept on board somehow that might cause us trouble at the frontier. We also stow away all our cold weather gear and make ready for more shorts and t-shirts.

Penny at least goes out on a high. Our paperwork for departing the Middle Kingdom is in impeccable order. We take one last photo of the three of us together before Penny has to hurry off to the bus station to catch the first in a long relay of buses back to Chengdu.

And then, it is time to say: *Zaijian, ZhongGuo!*

Laos, here we come.

TEN

———

Laos to Bangkok

Tom

Of all the border crossings we have now bickered, argued, bribed, pleaded and sweated our way through, none is more comically simple than our entry into Laos. We leave behind a gleaming steel and glass building symbolising all that is ordered and on the rise – even in this forgotten corner of China – and cross over to an outpost which amounts to barely more than a shack. We hand over the $20 fee for entry and are waved through with not an eyelid batted in our direction. Netty is not opened, let alone inspected or searched.

We drive away laughing at the beautiful simplicity of it.

Driving further into Laos, the scenery changes quickly and dramatically. Northern Laos is very rural and very poor. For someone who has watched far too many films about the Vietnam War, the landscape is rather familiar, too. Everything is lush and green and the limestone karst mountains spring up in sheer faces of rock apparently out of nowhere. The agrarian life in this remote region of the country is simple. Houses are made of wood or bamboo with woven bamboo roofs. All of them are propped up on stilts. This provides a shaded area under which each family can gather, as well as a dry place to store firewood.

The village folk stare at us as we drive past and we stare back: at children being bathed in steel bowls, at the womenfolk washing their clothes under a bamboo pipe feeding directly off the hillside, at menfolk weaving baskets sitting in the dust in the space under their houses and much more. To top it all, it being mid-May, many of the villages are surrounded by flowering bushes and trees on all sides. Everything appears wonderfully authentic and we are indeed a long way off the tourist trail here.

This point is somewhat worryingly illustrated as we drive through the mountains. Hicky is at the wheel, and as we round a bend on the side of a hill we see two kids standing by the side of the road. I imagine they were about thirteen or fourteen. Immediately something strikes me as wrong, although at first I don't realise what it is. Suddenly my conscious brain catches up with my subconscious and I shout to Hicky: 'Drive! Drive! Drive!' Confused but instantly responsive he puts his foot down and we disappear round the bend. The children had both been holding AK47s.

'Wow,' Hicky mutters. 'I clocked it just after you shouted. Why the hell were they holding those?'

'No idea – but I'm glad we aren't still there to find out!'

As darkness approaches we arrive in a small village where we soon find a bamboo hut overlooking the river. Cost – $5.

The intense heat and humidity require some getting used to. We are meeting my brother and Mima in Luang Prabang, a well-known French colonial town perched on a promontory marking the confluence of the Nam

Khan River with the mighty Mekong River. The place is beautifully serene and caters to the high-end tourist just as well as the gap-year backpacker, perhaps more so. Even now I think of it as one of the most lovely places I've ever been, complete with French colonial architecture, the ubiquitous Buddhist temples of this region and the colourful night markets which could surely amuse even the most recalcitrant tourist. I record in my journal that upon arrival, 'Hicky and I did a bit of recon prior to the others arriving and ended up rather drunk in the process.' A clear non-sequitur if you ask me, then again I have no reason to doubt that it is true.

The following day the others arrive.

We end up spending three delightful days in Luang Prabang, which is so idyllic that it proves a very hard place to leave. From here, our little company of four drive south to the town of Vang Vieng where we spend nearly five days, variously 'tube-ing' – a hazardous pursuit involving riding an inner tube down a river-rapid, which never fails to attract gap-year travellers – eating, drinking and generally making merry. This sequence of days is much more holiday than overland expedition and there is not a lot to report of major note, other than we were gradually eroding the distance between us and the city of Bangkok where we would be packing Netty in her final shipping container and sending her off to the big bad ole US of A.

There had been some debate whether we would complete this final leg of the journey, which would mean speeding our way across the United States at the height of summer. It is only really on arrival in Luang Prabang that we have fully committed to this course of action, the alternative being to call the trip at Bangkok and head back to London. Looking back, it seems crazy that we would ever *not* complete the circuit, as it were. And I'm very glad we did.

The final run into Bangkok is straightforward. We give ourselves things to do along the way – we visit a fabulous Angkor temple from which we can gaze out over the first valleys of Cambodia, we witness a huge colony of bats taking flight from rest to go hunting as the sun sets a deep orange over the western hills in very dramatic fashion.

The drama continues when at last we arrive in Bangkok. We happen to have turned up when bad things are happening: hardly a day before there has been a 'Red Demonstration' – when a crowd of republican/communist protesters burned down a shopping centre in the middle of the Thai capital. We are given to understand that this is in protest against the King of Thailand, though we are not sure exactly what about. The result is that a citywide curfew is in place for the first couple of days we are there and thus we are kept on a relatively short leash.

Nevertheless, once things settle down a bit, Hicky is at last able to deliver on the bet he made (and lost) back in Chengdu. (Something to do with the world's strongest Long Island Iced Tea.) To his credit, he is man to the task and treats all four of us to a slap-up dinner in the Mandarin Oriental.

This really puts the cap on our adventure to date. Our friends leave and, on June 2nd 2010, exactly seven months and twenty days after departing Parliament Square, we seal up Netty in her shipping container. Astonishingly, given the complications of our other shipping experiences, the Thai customs officials do not even bother to turn up. We later learn from our shipping agent that he has informed them that, having seen a list of what our car contained, he is sure that they would find a number of articles which would only generate more paperwork for them to deal with. This being the case, they shouldn't bother coming down. And they didn't.

Instead we kiss the old girl goodbye and tuck her up for her three-week journey across the mighty Pacific Ocean. We will not see her again until over five weeks later at LAX airport in the sunshine state of California.

ELEVEN

Coast to Coast – Coming in to Land

Hicky

With Netty steaming her way across the salty deep towards the sunny climes of California, we enjoy a sojourn of about a month in Thailand and then Vietnam, styling ourselves backpackers rather than overlanders for a while. We see plenty and continue to have an interesting time, but the restrictions on one's freedom – not being able to go and see more or less exactly what we like – mean that we are fairly itching to be back in the Netster once our plane touches down at LAX.

In fact, we beat her to the other side of the Pacific by just over a week. We spend the week as one might in LA – being put up by some generous but tenuous contacts, partying in Malibu or 'the Hills' by night, trawling around the sights of Hollywood by day, spotting the odd celeb, and generally entering into the rather louche lifestyle on offer. There are also a few World Cup games to watch although England have already been ignominiously despatched in the first days of the tournament so even that holds little interest.

Thus, we are relieved and eager to get going when we at

last learn that the Netster has landed. Sadly, this is no cue for immediate launch. Instead, it takes us another week to negotiate her release from LAX customs. True to their officious nature, US Customs decide that the container in which Netty arrives needs an 'intensive exam'. This means a US$1,000 bill for us – a bitter pill to swallow, the taste of which is in no way improved when we discover our GPS device has been stolen from the glove box in the course of their 'intensive' inspection.

'Where's Aubrey when you need him?' I lament to Tom as we drive away.

Having had our fill of LA for the time being, we nevertheless set out in high spirits for the first port of call on our meandering (but rather rapid) route across the States: Yosemite National Park. We have armed ourselves with a weighty yellow pages guide listing every campsite in America which will prove to be worth its weight in gold. And indeed, being back on the camping trail evokes happy (if distant) memories of those first days on the road through western Europe at the start of our journey. Except here, we will be camping in the warm.

Yosemite is a place of extraordinary natural beauty – as any who have visited there will attest. The austere grandeur of El Capitan and Half Dome mountain, the ethereal majesty of the Bridalveil Fall, the valleys carpeted with sequoia trees and pines, the rock pools, the dusty hiking trails, the verdant meadows bursting with life, the cosy lodges, the immaculately manicured camping parks all create in us a sincere appreciation for Theodore Roosevelt and his determination to preserve the best of the American landscape with his system of national parks. We sleep, we walk, we swim, we eat, we walk some more, and suck down the fulsome fresh air, feeling lucky to be on the home straight and surrounded by such beauty.

A swan song then, and one we fully intend to make the most of.

Tom

From the sublime to the ridiculous – or at least the insufferable – as we head a couple of hundred miles south-east into Death Valley in the Mojave Desert. Google weather tells us that the mercury is going to hit fifty-two degrees Celsius today as we plunge down into the swelter, passing sign after sign reminding us to check our air-con is in working order.

'Air-con? Are they joking?' laughs Hicky.

Clearly, the highway officials of California are not familiar with the long wheelbase Land Rover. The Netster is equipped with a very under-powered heater-fan, incapable of relieving so much as a single bead of sweat in such conditions. In fact, the opposite is the case. We have to drop to 30mph and turn *up* the heater to full blast in order to suck the hot air away from the engine to prevent Netty from over-heating. We, meanwhile, are forced to strip down to our underpants, sweat pouring off us in rivers.

The landscape is extraordinary but in a very different way – a moonscape of dust and rock, heat and sand, jagged wind-sculpted ripples of rock jut out of the earth, the air shimmers like a grid-iron above the perfect strip of black tarmac. Out of curiosity, we pull over at the deepest part of the valley, some eighty-six metres below sea level, and crack an egg on the tarmac. Dutifully it sizzles away. A five-dollar bet is won and lost, though I forget in whose favour.

Looking around, I confess to feeling a little daunted by the sheer inhospitality of the place and find myself thinking back to the vast range of conditions to which we have subjected the Netster. From the Tibetan high plateau to this. I am glad when we press on into the state of Nevada although we damn nearly don't make it over the final crest to get out of the valley. With Netty pushed to her absolute limit and deep into the red zone of her temperature gauge it is with some relief that we let her freewheel (and cool down) on the downhill road towards the border town of Beatty where we break for lunch.

Bizarre as this place is, with gamblers of every description frequenting its diners and casinos, and aside from stopping for a plateful of food that would have bloated a bear for a week, we cannot dally. Because, as so many have done before us, we are heading for Las Vegas.

The bright lights and the gaudy billboards and the glittering hotel facades and the flamboyant fountains and the sleek stretched limousines with their blacked-out windows, the dust and the dingy bars and the greasy diners and the ugly people and the stink of money (not to mention the ill-advised personal life choices being made at any given moment) – it is all there in Vegas. We draw into town exactly nine months after our departure from London. This time, I am fully ready to embrace Hicky's many film references which spill out of him like coins from a slot-machine. Foremost among these is *The Hangover* – a by-now cult film about a stag-party in Vegas released not long before our trip. The protagonists stay in Caesar's Palace; therefore we stay in 'Caesar's Palache' (as we are soon calling it).

There follows twenty-four hours which cannot, in fairness to our reputations, be reported in these pages.

The one thing I would like to stress, however, is that we didn't get married.

Hicky
It is doubtless a very good thing that we leave the next day in search of the purity that only raw nature can afford. We are heading for perhaps the most iconic natural feature of all: the Grand Canyon.

Neither of us remember the drive too well since of more immediate concern are the hammer-drills working at the inside of our skulls. It is more of a scurry to the canyon rim than a triumphal progress, despite the fact that we cross the impressive Hoover Dam on the way. We spend the first night in a campsite just outside the main national park, imposing on ourselves an early curfew and a strict no alcohol policy (for one night only).

Come morning, I scrabble together some fried corn and noodles after which we begin to feel ready to tackle this monster. It is a glorious, clear, hot day. But instead of hiking down into the canyon we follow an eight-mile trail along its rim, enjoying the breathtakingly epic views out across the vast expanse of stratigraphic majesty that falls away below us. We are bemused by the nasty officiousness with which the bus driver berates us for standing up in our seats on the ride to the head of the rim trail. Once on the trail there's not so much as a handrail to prevent hikers from plunging to their death several thousand feet below. Such is the paradox of American health and safety.

The canyon itself has to be seen to be believed, far exceeding any expectations I might have had. The vast emptiness of the landscape impresses itself upon you – even in these more touristic places. The awesome silence and the extraordinary scale of the monumental rock formations that rise up out of the desert. We spend the next day effectively driving around the whole canyon, leapfrogging from Flagstaff to Cameron to Bitter Springs and north to Zion National Park. (We have crossed from Arizona into Utah now.) There we camp, though it is so hot upon arrival that we can hardly move around the campsite without becoming exhausted, let alone embark on a lengthy trek. In the cool of the morning, however, we walk down into the canyon, hike around and then climb up out again. Part of our walk takes us across one ridge-line known as Angels Landing, a rock formation with a perilously narrow path cut along it with a thousand-foot drop-off on either side. The reward for braving this rather precipitous route is a view out (from Angels Landing itself) over the Zion canyon. The day is exhilarating, to say the least.

From Zion we head north on Route 15, turn east on Route 70 at the improbably named Sulphurdale, then push on another hundred and sixty miles to Green River. From there, we begin to see the mighty Rocky Mountains rising up ahead of us. We decide to repast in a well-known local watering hole called Ray's Tavern. As we enter, the music stops and everyone in the joint turns to look at us. A little disconcerting perhaps, but then one had got used to that sort of thing on the road down from Lhasa. We leave feeling once more soiled to our very souls with the mountains of food forced upon us.

From here on in, the distances start getting pretty massive. We are pushing for the finish line and quite happy to truck along for upwards of ten hours a day. From the plains of Green River, we intend to clear the Rocky Mountains in all their summer glory in one hit. Route 70 takes us through Grand Junction, climbs up to

Vail, where we stop and spend an afternoon mountain biking – which was less fun than I had hoped and gained me little but a sore arse.

From Vail to Denver is less than a hundred miles. By the time you reach it, the Rockies have vanished as quickly as they appeared. Beyond the Mile High City lie almost exactly a thousand miles of plain and prairie along Route 80, until you reach Chicago and the Great Lakes. We chew up just about half of this in one hit, reaching as far as Lincoln, Nebraska before we pull off the road to camp. A distance of 608 miles in one day. A personal best.

The end is in sight. We pass the long weary miles across the Great American Plain talking about everything we have experienced, reflecting on what it will be like to get home, on what we might do. Meanwhile Middle America flashes by, thousands of acres of soya beans and wheat and maize – the breadbasket of the American staple diet. If our own experience is anything to go by, most of it will end up in the garbage. A typical day would be to drive for ten hours with a brief stop in the middle for a burger the size of Belgium, a small heart attack and two gallons of Pepsi before wearily trundling into a local campsite for the night. Entering the outer limits of Lincoln, we pass a twenty-foot-high white cross.

'Great rig, man,' says one fellow RV wanderer, once we've parked up in the campsite just off the freeway.

Apparently the Land Rover Defender is a rarity in the US, it being almost impossible to import.

'Couldn't agree more,' says Tom. The man will never know why.

After that it's Des Moines, Iowa; then a grotty city campsite next to an amusement park in Cleveland, Ohio. And finally, our last night.

Tom

Some eighty-five miles out from New York, still on Route 80 (of which we have become rather fond), we pull into our last campsite somewhere just outside the little town of Stroudsburg, Pennsylvania. Being a small place, the campsite is more or less deserted. We settle down in a quiet spot where, having procured ourselves a bottle of bubbly and a few bottles of red going by the name of 'Smoking Loon', we proceed to celebrate circumnavigating the globe.

Smoking Loon, it turns out, proves an entirely apt name on which to end, since what unfolds has something of the lunatic in it. A kind of feral Bacchanalian wildness takes hold of us both. (Happily there is no one around to see it.) We drink, we dance, we cry to the moon, we leap all over Netty, we head-bang, we tear around in the dark in the woods, we strip half-naked and beat our bare chests. It's all very Lord of the Flies and, I suppose, marks a suitably free-spirited end to this most epic of journeys. For any who think this is just exaggerated hyperbole there are, I'm afraid, rather a lot of photos that can prove otherwise.

It is July 24th 2010. We drive the last couple of hours into New York subdued but deeply satisfied. We have covered a distance of 25,432 miles in the nine months and eleven days since pulling away from Parliament Square on October 13th of last year. Three continents, twenty-five countries. In the end, saying goodbye to Netty is a simple affair. The drop-off is an address in New Jersey. We pack her up, put her to bed, sign the necessary paperwork and away we go.

'Well, my friend,' I say to Hickman as our taxi is pulling away. 'We said we'd wing it…'

'And wing it, we did.'

Epilogue

Home Again

Hicky

I write this on 3rd November 2020 in the midst of the COVID-19 pandemic, as the second UK lockdown approaches. The world is mostly in a similar state, and people can only imagine what it is like to travel to remote and magical places, meeting people from all walks of life and experiencing cultures far from our own.

When Tom and I left on that blustery October day in 2009 the world was also in a state of flux. We were deeply curious, but for us that world had up till then remained largely unexplored, having grown up within a small bubble, albeit brought up to appreciate people, nature and culture. What we learned was that moving out of your comfort zone and using your innate curiosity to see differently was something very important.

What touched me most was the kindness we experienced. An age of perpetual, and mostly negative, news produces a misguided view of how people in other cultures are. Along our travels we rarely experienced anything other than genuine kindness and curiosity in us, what we were doing, and where we came from. As the world begins to open up, I can only encourage anyone who has the opportunity to do something similar to grab it (and wing it!). Trust me, you won't regret it.

Tom

The idea of a big adventure had been brewing in me for a number of years. I absolutely love to travel and I enjoy a challenge, so the thought of combining the two was irresistible. However, this could so easily have remained a pipe dream. Our drunken conversation at the top of a mountain could so easily have remained just that. We all have good ideas that never quite find form.

What I take most pride in is simply the fact that Hicky and I made the trip happen at all. There were countless good reasons not to do it. A thousand reasons to delay. And we ignored them all.

We had no real experience, we didn't have the first clue about car mechanics, Hicky had never 'travelled' before and, barring a couple of dates in our diary, we had no plans for our year away. None of it mattered. We winged the entire thing and it was the best decision of my life to date.

On return to the UK it was time to face the reality of a career. Oh so nearly did I return to the consulting world I knew, but at the last moment an idea presented itself in the form of yet another, somewhat inebriated, conversation with a great friend. Would I have gone for it without the confidence gained from a year away or the sense of freedom and opportunity it left behind? Who knows, but I'd like to think it played a part. It led to another equally unusual and totally different adventure.

One thing is for sure, our trip has had a lasting impact on both of us and to me it has been a source of great comfort and perspective over the years that have followed.

As we emerge from the global COVID pandemic, affected in ways I suspect we do not yet fully appreciate, it is a reminder of just how important it is to seize these chances and make them a reality. Carpe Diem, YOLO, *one life, live it* – take your pick.

Netty

A bittersweet postscript to this story. Having braved over 25,000 miles in our care without so much as a flat tyre, our trusty Netty was stolen from outside Tom's house in Norfolk in late November 2010. The irony of this, after all she had overcome, was a hard pill to swallow. In desperation we went to the *Eastern Daily Press* (the main regional newspaper) who agreed to publish an article covering the story. Meanwhile, we were heartbroken … for about three weeks.

The happy last word is this: an observant officer of the Norfolk Constabulary happened to pull up behind Netty at a set of traffic lights in Norwich and, recognising her from the recent *EDP* article, was able to recover her from her captors and return her to our safekeeping just in time for Christmas.

Needless to say, there was much rejoicing. This was neatly described in the *EDP*'s follow-up article, where 'a source' was quoted saying that Hicky 'squealed like a little girl at Christmas' when told of her rescue. He is still trying to track down the source…